I0019812

Joo Hwan Lee

Evaluating the Interactivity of Ubiquitous Services

Joo Hwan Lee

Evaluating the Interactivity of Ubiquitous Services

An Integrated Metric Based on UCD (User-Centered Design) Principles

VDM Verlag Dr. Müller

Imprint

Bibliographic information by the German National Library: The German National Library lists this publication at the German National Bibliography; detailed bibliographic information is available on the Internet at http://dnb.d-nb.de.

Cover image: www.purestockx.com

Published 2008 Saarbrücken

Publisher:
VDM Verlag Dr. Müller Aktiengesellschaft & Co. KG , Dudweiler Landstr. 125 a,
66123 Saarbrücken, Germany,
Phone +49 681 9100-698, Fax +49 681 9100-988,
Email: info@vdm-verlag.de

Produced in Germany by:
Reha GmbH, Dudweilerstrasse 72, D-66111 Saarbrücken
Schaltungsdienst Lange o.H.G., Zehrensdorfer Str. 11, 12277 Berlin, Germany
Books on Demand GmbH, Gutenbergring 53, 22848 Norderstedt, Germany

Impressum

Bibliografische Information der Deutschen Nationalbibliothek: Die Deutsche Nationalbibliothek verzeichnet diese Publikation in der Deutschen Nationalbibliografie; detaillierte bibliografische Daten sind im Internet über http://dnb.d-nb.de abrufbar.

Coverbild: www.purestockx.com

Erscheinungsjahr: 2008
Erscheinungsort: Saarbrücken

Verlag: VDM Verlag Dr. Müller Aktiengesellschaft & Co. KG , Dudweiler Landstr. 125 a,
D- 66123 Saarbrücken,
Telefon +49 681 9100-698, Telefax +49 681 9100-988,
Email: info@vdm-verlag.de

Herstellung in Deutschland:
Schaltungsdienst Lange o.H.G., Zehrensdorfer Str. 11, D-12277 Berlin
Books on Demand GmbH, Gutenbergring 53, D-22848 Norderstedt
Reha GmbH, Dudweilerstrasse 72, D-66111 Saarbrücken

ISBN: 978-3-639-02908-6

Table of contents

Tables

Figures

Part I: Introduction

1. Introduction

1.1 Background and problem definition

The term 'ubiquitous computing' means 'computing exists everywhere' and this represents the direction of the changes and development in computing that have become prominent in the 2000s (Norman, 1999). A diverse newly-composed word was used in a mixture and the concept of the word was expanded to the concept of 'Everyware' comprising the characteristics of computer hardware and software to represent the terms of ubiquitous computing (Greenfield, 2006). Also, the services in ubiquitous computing environments changed the subjects of marketing strategies from developers to users. They became the temporal background underlying the changes in design environments from old service development-oriented ones to user communication-oriented ones. That is, 'consumers' as 'users' have come to emerge as principal actors to create changes in today's societies along with their great influences. Consequently, the interactions between ubiquitous services and users have come to take an important position in ubiquitous industry and new approaches to practical evaluations are required due to the emergences of many unverified services.

The connection between the computers built in many place or location and the mobile information devices constitute ubiquitous computing environments. Humans surrounded by environments become to use multiple computers anywhere at any time and the services provided in ubiquitous environments attempt to provide optimum services by perceiving the behaviors and intentions of users. Environmental characteristics are different from other forms of services obtained from using computers because the computers connected in many different places or locations attempt to imitate the service

1

patterns made in the relationships of users in order to support users' behaviors. Also, whereas existing methods to use computers require active efforts to select suitable devices among diverse types of computers and to execute supporting programs in order to achieve their necessary goals, the users in ubiquitous computing environments can be naturally provided with necessary services without any requirement. The difference in concepts necessitates the changes in paradigms in terms of the context of use and the quality of use and/or usability (Heckmann, 2005).

Especially, ubiquitous computing environments attempt to build up not only the existing method that supports services on requests but also the service system that will grasp the intentions and context of users to actively support, and this conceptual approach is defined as ubiquitous service or u-Service (Holtjona and Fiona, 2004; Lee, 2006). That is, ubiquitous services can appropriately develop user context considering past behavioral patterns of environments and can provide necessary information and resources to users anywhere. Analyzing individuals' experiences to provide customized (tailored) services, ubiquitous services can be said to have become unique interactions with humans and life styles rather than just technologies or tools (Abowd and Mynatt, 2000).

Since 2005, many newly develpoed words utilizing the term 'ubiquitous' as a noun have emerged in IT (Information Technology) industry and 'u-Korea', 'u-Government', 'u-Society', 'u-City', and 'u-Business' are used in the same way as general service terms are used (Jo et al., 2006). However, up to date, the researches related to ubiquitous computing have been centered on fundamental technologies, standardization and security and the researches on the services newly emerging in ubiquitous environments are quite insufficient, thus the concept or classification of ubiquitous services has not been firmly established (Aarts and Marzano, 2003). But the ultimate shape of ubiquitous services to be eventually pursued means the provision of the computing environments with the concept of 'utility' where services can be used freely and easily like electricity or service water (Lyytinen and Yoo, 2002). This environmental change became a great motive for the expansion of researches into Human-Computer Interaction (HCI), and it is rapidly changing the researches related to mobile (mobile HCI), rapidly developed after the year of 2000, into the researches related to ubiquitous (ubiquitous HCI) (Hull et al., 2002; Langheinrich, 2002).

The emergence of ubiquitous services that has been transformed into the arena of state-of-the-art is being fingered as a cause adding the economic burden to users due to temporary services neglecting the requirements of users and silo-approach services at the convenience of service providers. Commenced to overcome that vicious circle, the approach to large-scaled projects related to diverse ubiquitous services initially brought about from communications among humans as well as between humans and computers. Moreover the theological and technological advancements of service designs to support collaborations between users (Resnick, 2001; Takemoto et al., 2002; Blaine et al., 2005) and activated user studies relating to the selections of ubiquitous services (service matching or selection method) issues for the provision of the services complying with implicit needs of users focusing on the human factors such as usability, service-awareness, and trust, etc. (Lindenberg et al., 2007). On the other hand, it brought about visual advancements in complex viewpoints such as the performances of diverse components for the evaluation of the levels and qualities of ubiquitous services that have been progressing in many places, system usability and interactions between users and systems (Williams, 2004; Byun, 2005). This expansion of ubiquitous industry scope resulted in the need of the development of the techniques that will enable the evaluation of state-of-the-art and diversified ubiquitous services from the user-centered views (Brinkman et al., 2007).

Especially, as an approach to the evaluation of the levels and qualities of ubiquitous services, a small number of researchers attempted to apply an evaluation methodology using an extension of existing service quality evaluation technique, an application of software quality evaluation technique and usability among core concepts of User-

3

Centered Design (UCD). Nevertheless these approaches revealed its limitation by origin of a partial evaluation technique that could not reflect the characteristics of ubiquitous services on appropriate places or locations and evaluated only specific components of ubiquitous services. That is, excluding the key attributes such as experience, motivation and engagement or immersion given importance in ubiquitous service, these approaches grafted existing service evaluation techniques to ubiquitous environments, and thereby it had the limitation that it could not evaluate the nature of ubiquitous services (Iqbal et al., 2005).

1.2 Purpose and scope of the study

Ubiquitous services aim at providing users with the optimum services by adapting context changes in the requirements of users. Although the goals are attractive, it is not guaranteed that users will necessarily experience the ubiquitous services as attractive and satisfactory. Ubiquitous services are not only premised on the introduction of new environments different from existing physical spaces, but also will bring about new kinds of interactions different from existing relations thus the contents and patterns of the ubiquitous services experienced by users contain the possibility to be developed differently from those as expected (Roussos and Moussouri, 2004). Therefore, the complexity of the contents provided to users through ubiquitous services is to be suggested as the concept of human-system interaction capability (hereinafter, interactivity) which is the expansion of the concept of usability and is introduced into the methods of ubiquitous service evaluations in order to emphasize the relationships between services and users rather than to distinguish them.

The methods and techniques of service evaluation are diversified but this research aims at the development of the service evaluation methods reflecting the characteristics of interactions that are given importance in ubiquitous environments, in order to overcome the fact that the evaluation methods considering ubiquitous environmental characteristics are being applied fragmentarily like the expansion of computing environments. The suggested approach is considered to be a important research evaluating the services involving users' subjective measurements from the viewpoint of interactivity in order to expand the user-centered design approach that has been studied from the past.

This research aims at the development of interactivity metric reflecting the characteristics of ubiquitous services. Detailed goals of this research are as follows.

First, existing ubiquitous service evaluation methodologies are reviewed to define the evaluation attributes for ubiquitous service evaluations.

Second, user-centered interactive metrics that can overcome the limitations of those service evaluation methodologies, such as personal service evaluation methods, usability evaluation techniques and psychometrics based evaluation techniques, are to be developed.

Third, the ubiquitous service interactivity metric developed is to be realized as systems so that it can be readily applied to designers, developers and users.

Through these goals, the attributes focused in designing ubiquitous services are to be defined as user-centered factors which are to be subsequently evaluated by applying the methods that measure realized service even at low levels.

However, the methods to realize ubiquitous services are much diversified thus the contents about the methods to realize the services or the technical evaluation methods (middleware quality, system configuration, wireless networks, etc.) are excluded from the scope of this research.

1.3 Methodology to the study

In order to resolve the issues of how to conceptualize and evaluate the interactivity of ubiquitous services, the development of new concepts to consider both of the aspect of the usability of services and the aspect of personal services for users is required. Thus the method to explore various aspects related to ubiquitous services, and then to systematically refine more central factors from them will be utilized. The compositeness of ubiquitous services will be concretely revealed and it will be checked if ubiquitous services have the multi-dimensional property which would not be recognized or predicted to be simple combinations of existing usability or service qualities.

A critical success factors in this approach is that the psychological dimensions experienced by users should also be extracted through complete ubiquitous services rather than the technology level of the services. Psychometric theory was utilized to do such measurement and since measurement variables themselves are not psychological attributes, latent variables were composed using the responses obtained through measurement variables to correspond the latent variables to the methods describing the relations between concepts with latent variables (Nunnally and Bernstein, 1994). Especially, since ubiquitous services not only distribute large numbers of diverse types of devices but also aim at the invisible services filtered into environments. The problem of subjects being increased in number or becoming obscure arises thus the evaluations of particular devices (artifacts) are limited, and the questions for measurements of the quality of personal services do not reflect the characteristics of ubiquitous services. Considering these limitations, this study attempted to develop the evaluation questions reflecting the characteristics of ubiquitous services. When evaluation tools were developed based on traditional psychometric theory, the tools were developed by observing user's responses to the experiences in subjects (Pyun, 2005). However, the evaluations are limited because there were not so many ubiquitous services that users can experience. Consequently, if the services that can be experienced firsthand are not available, the evaluations of interactivity become challenges that cannot be easily solved. This study attempted to explore the attributes of ubiquitous services experienced by users, and to integrate the factors extracted from the researches into interactivity and service qualities in order to develop the pool of user-centered evaluation factors. Developed factors were refined and the basic items of the interactivity evaluation metrics for user-

6

centered ubiquitous services were extracted.

This study consists of five parts as below (figure 1).

Part I shows the goals of this study, problem definitions, the scope of study and approaches.

Part II, as examinations of related researches, the contents of newest researches related to ubiquitous service and interactivity were reviewed, and the researches related to Usability Evaluation Methodology (UEM) and service evaluations were examined. Also, the evaluation methods utilizing User-Centered Design (UCD) and research cases and the evaluation methodology utilizing psychometrics were reviewed.

Part III, the factors for the interactivity evaluation of ubiquitous services were collected and extracted. Each attribute was extracted and factors were structuralized through expert examinations, and correlations between one another were analyzed. Also, questionnaires were developed based on extracted factors to execute direct evaluations. Statistics analyses such as reliability analyses were executed in order to correct factors. In case studies, the ubiquitous services (u-Home services) currently being provided was executed to verify the evaluation metric developed. Finally, the metrics were completed by interactivity index and the tool to automate metric was developed.

Part IV shows the conclusion and contributions of this study.

Part V contains the literature review data and basic statistic results (principal component analysis, correspondence analysis) used in this study.

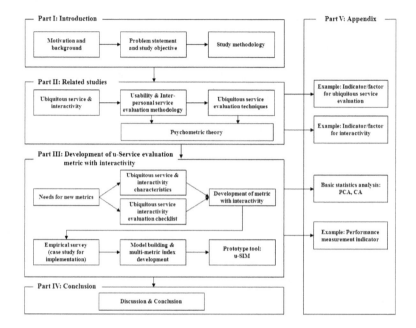

Figure 1. Structure of this study

Part II: Related studies

2. Background theories and literature reviews

The evaluation modeling for the interactivity of ubiquitous services can be approached from three main aspects. First, the viewpoint believing that interactivity is the result of the use of ubiquitous services. Since ubiquitous services are the result of the responses, the approach from the aspect of existing usability (ease of use, quality of use) researches is practicable. Second, since ubiquitous services are also inter-personal services, the approach regarding the evaluations of the quality of inter-personal services is possible. The approach is possible from the evaluation of satisfaction aspect of the service quality such as service system performances or the kindness of service providers. Third, the method to evaluate the quality of inter-personal services are related to the satisfaction as it is perceived by users, efforts and prides rather than the dichotomy between success and/or failure thus the approach from such aspect of affective evaluation is also possible. This approach is possible only when the psychological dimensions of the experience of interactions with users are extracted.

2.1 Research related to human-system interaction capability (interactivity) with ubiquitous services

If there is no particular model about what the shape of future blueprint will be, the development of ubiquitous services will lose motivations. Also, ubiquitous service evaluations should be modeled from the viewpoint of users rather than the viewpoint of developers. Since there has been no attempt to evaluate ubiquitous services from the viewpoint of users, the evaluation system for users' interactivity necessary to achieve the goals of this study cannot be easily formalized. Therefore, the model for the evaluation of the interactivity of user-centered ubiquitous services is to be approached from two aspects.

The first is that the interactivity of ubiquitous services is the result of the use of ubiquitous services. This means the researches into usability that has been evaluated to be a key factor in user-centered design can be adapted. The second is that ubiquitous services also model the activities of service servant in inter-personal services. Therefore, the former can be approached from the aspect of usability and the latter can be approached from the aspect of the researches regarding the quality of inter-personal services.

Ubiquitous services are also called as 'the servants (group) that collect and share information to help their masters (Bellotti and Sellen, 1993; Bellotti et al., 2002)' and the servants, in order to provide the services satisfactory to their masters, read the faces of their masters and exchange or share necessary information with each other, and wait for proper times to provide services. Here, servants mean 'context-awareness enabled computing devices' and they should be connected with each other and be monitoring the situations of their masters all the time everywhere to provide necessary supports. This status is called 'ubiquity'. Also, the information shared among information technologies should always be updated to the newest ones and the optimum user information through comparisons with error information for customized services should be accumulated. This is called 'self-growing (Schmidt, 2002)'. The researches related to these definitions of the attributes of ubiquitous services are to be reviewed.

2.1.1 Ubiquitous service related researches

Ubiquitous service related researches are basically purposed to enable users to concentrate on the works they intend to do as well as to enhance work efficiencies. Nowadays, it is difficult to predict what influences the emergence of ubiquitous

10

technology will bring onto businesses except it is obvious that the applications of ubiquitous technologies are developing quietly around us. Active discussions and researches about ubiquitous service for state-of-the-art are emerging as major issues (Schmidt, 2003-b).

The key area of researches related to computing have been largely divided into the area of the development of wireless networks aiming at speeding up connections of computers, embedding of functions and the methods to miniaturize devices enhancing portability to concentrate technological developments (Steitz et al., 2001). Also, the necessity of researches into context-awareness as a core technology in diverse applied services was the highlight (Barton and Kindberg, 2001; Barkhuus and Dey, 2003).

Besides the technological view, the ubiquitous services from the viewpoint of inter-personal services are simply putting into common everyday products (ISO 20282, 2006). For example, the computers are suitable to the roles of each one to enable the things to communicate with each other (Device To Device: D2D). This is because the concepts and range of applications are not restricted to limited ranges but expanded to daily life spaces and the areas invisible in human eyes. For this, many researches focused researches into ubiquitous services on the development of context-awareness models. Through hierarchical researches involving context-awareness, situation-awareness, and environment-awareness, where some researchers argued that system middleware was the most important key technology to active responses of ubiquitous services (Burnett and Rainsford, 2001; Bartram and Czerwinski, 2002; Arnstein et al., 2006). The concept of ubiquitous services (u-Services) can be understood to be the concept that mixes the inherent information based on ubiquity and the characteristic of ubiquitous provisions. Thereby it starts from the extensions of electronic services (e-Services) along with mobile services (m-Services) to include both concepts, then at the same time to expand the methods and scopes of information devices, networks and commercial transactions (Leonard et al., 2002; table 1).

Table 1. Changes in service concepts with changes in environments

Terms	Concepts	Tools
Service	A set of actions, processes and results that changes products, information, etc. from a state to another state with the participation of customers.	Face to face contact, Inter-personal service
e-Service	An electronic service that improves efficiency of internal works of organizations and enhance customer support processes.	Value added networks, Internet, Computer
m-Service	A mobile service that delivers e-Services through mobile devices to overcome temporal and spatial restrictions.	Communication network, Handheld devices, PDA
u-Service	A real time service that enables users to access to wanted information any time anywhere as needed by individuals with intelligent service.	Wireless network, Sensor, Tag, Portable or invisible terminal

But the concepts of services currently used in common are applied much more comprehensively than these definitions, and boundaries between each other are becoming obscurer. With rapid developments of information technologies and for the satisfaction of diverse consumer demands, the scope is also expanded. And, understanding the human beings and services obviously has to research human attention, intention, behavior, preference and so on. On the other hand, 'what are services?' is still a major issue (Heikkinen and Porras, 2005). Without understanding services, many researches can not determine the most appropriate service in some situation. Many technologies for service description are proposed so far, but many researches do not know whether they are enough or not (Heikkinen, 2005).

In the research of Snowden and Kurtz (2002) and IBM (2007), the difficulty of understanding ubiquitous services was explained as the difference between 'complicated service' and 'complex service'. The complicated service means the service constructs that diverse services are gathered but can be distinguished, and the complex service is defined as a service. Diverse services are gathered to realize synergies between services and symbiosis (interdependency) thus the conceptual approach to the provision of completely different attributes as a service was attempted.

Yamazaki (2004) defined Ubiquitous Computing Environment (UCE) which is an enormous number of RFID tags, sensors, and other heterogeneous small devices will be embedded in the real world, and services provided by UCE 'ubiquitous service'. Comparing with existing services typically provided by the internet, ubiquitous services have the following characteristics: 1) Services are provided, or often triggered, based on physical conditions, 2) Since services are invoked when such conditions are satisfied, services know the state-of-the-world and users context, 3) Services are provided when a user is not expecting conscious them, because they are triggered automatically by the service system but not by the user's intention.

As for the researches related to ubiquitous service attributes, limited researches centered on the concepts for the developments of products and/or services in mobile (real time online) environments preceded this research (Stanford, 2002; Morikawa and Aoyama, 2004; Markett et al., 2006). Kannan et al. (2001) expressed the property of mobile services as 'ubiquitous interactivity' and suggested the fact that interactivities among humans, between humans and machines are possible anytime anywhere as one of their characteristics. Lee (2003) defined the multi-dimensional attributes of interactivity as 'user controllability', 'responsiveness', 'personalization', 'connectivity', 'ubiquity', and 'context-awareness' through integrated approaches to the interactivity of mobile environments and suggested systems for the development of mobile services.

To establish clear concepts between mobile and ubiquitous, researches related to 'mobility (Skiba et al., 2000)', 'accessibility', 'location-awareness (Buckler and Buxel, 2000)', and 'identification (Muller, 1999)' as the properties of mobile services differentiated from internet services, and in relation to the concepts constituting ubiquitous services differentiated from mobile services, researches related to the attributes such as 'ubiquity', 'universal', 'uniqueness', and 'unison' etc. were attempted (Da Costa and Punie, 2003).

13

Table 2. Ubiquitous service classification system in users' perspective (modified from Chung, 2005)

Classification criteria	Methods classification	Description
Utilization area	Living	Enhancement of convenience in living on the aspect of individuals.
	Working	Enhancement of work efficiency on the aspects of companies and countries.
Realization methods	Portable	Ubiquitous environments are realized through the computing devices as small as reasonably can be carried in hands.
	Embedded	Computing functions are embedded in environments to function while people do not perceive them.
Methods to use	Control	The service type where decisions should be made from the standpoints of users.
	Smart	The service that does not require separate decision making of users.

Also, researches that analyzed the properties of ubiquitous service environments in connection with the service classification system in the perspective of users were attempted. There was an attempt to classify ubiquitous services based on the classification criteria composed of three axes (utilization area, realization methods, and methods to use) (Chung, 2005; table 2).

Recently, the efforts to provide services by analyzing the behaviors of ubiquitous users were made. The researches related to Ubiquitous User Modeling (UUM) were mainly executed by Heckmann (2005) where he focused on how to minimize user interferences by causing systems and environments to share user models in the services used every day by users who do not perceive IT systems in living. He considered the sustained use of services through minimization of user interferences (unobtrusiveness) to be the key factor in ubiquitous service environments, proposing a method to develop the systems to realize unobtrusiveness services.

14

Especially, in 'airport scenario' research (figure 2), he modeled user behaviors in order to develop ubiquitous services. Thereby he proposed a method to conceptualize the complex processes of situated interactions for the method where service systems share user modeling and suggested a methodology for context-awareness user modeling (Want et al., 2002; Horvitz et al., 2003).

Also researches into the concept of 'Everyware' that defined ubiquitous computing as a paradigm related to the aspect of interactions between humans and computers (Greenfield, 2006). In Everyware, the conceptual approach to the ability to access to all information in the methods suitable for appropriate locations or situations was attempted. The researchers advocated the development of the services that would focus major properties of ubiquitous services on the establishment of the strategies for the increase of user experiences and the reduction of cognitive loads of users. Table 3 shows major researches into ubiquitous service attribute factors and dimensions.

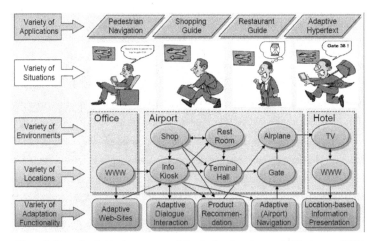

Figure 2. Example of ubiquitous user modeling in the airport scenario (Heckmann, 2005)

2.1.2 Researches into interactivity in ubiquitous environments

(1) Researches into interactivity in the area of HCI

Interaction means exchanging activities, i.e. the acts of persons or things exchanging influences with each other. Interactivity is generally understood as acts or reciprocal behavioral processes between two or more users in interactions and the media providing the possibility of these behaviors are referred to as interactivity (Lombard and Snyder-Dutch, 2001).

Diverse opinions were presented about the necessity and importance of researches on interactivity. Cho and Leckenby (1999) and Wu (1999) elucidated positive relations of interactivity between services and users with the attitudes of users, and defined the roles of interactivity as the efforts on online companies attempting to build up good relations with customers by telling them as the level of interactivity of webs would be enhanced, the companies would become more attractive. However, despite the fact there were the researches indicating that interactivity does not exert significant influences on customer satisfaction and the researches indicating that interactivity exerts rather negative effects on customer satisfaction (Novak et al., 2000).

Also, many researches pointed out that the explorations for the improvement of interactivity would lead next generation technological developments and presented two core characteristics of interactivity as user control and information exchange (Ha and James, 1998).

Table 3. Major researches into ubiquitous service attribute factors and dimensions

Researcher	Ubiquitous service attribute	Major research subject	Characteristics
Kannan et al. (2001)	Interactivity of ubiquitous, Individuality, Location-awareness.	The issues at the level of marketing related to mobile commerce.	Suggestion of the concepts for each attribute.
Lyytinen and Yoo (2002)	Embedment, Mobility.	Direction of IT in ubiquitous environments.	Ubiquitous computing, networks.
Junglas and Watson (2003)	Ubiquity, Inherence, Universality, Uniformity.	Development of ubiquitous commerce services.	Summarization of the attributes of ubiquitous commerce services.
BenMoussa (2004)	Convenience, Personalization, Ubiquity, Accessibility, Location-awareness, Instant accessibility.	Property classification for mobile commerce service.	Conceptual suggestion of the major service properties in mobile environments.
Chun and Pyun (2004)	Convenience in carrying, Linkage, Online support, Remote control, Product warranty, Functionality.	Concept of ubiquitous services.	Studied the general service attributes that defined the properties of ubiquitous services.
Chung (2005)	Portability, Embedment, Ease of operation, Intelligence.	The frameworks for the developments living type, working type services are provided.	Ubiquitous service classification in the perspective of users.
Heckmann (2005)	Minimization of user interferences, Constant carefulness (unobtrusiveness).	Scenario based ubiquitous service user modeling.	Research into the realization of Ubiquitous User Modeling (UUM).
Greenfield (2006)	User experience, Accessibility, Reduction of cognitive loads.	Ambient informatics.	Defined Everyware services and extracted properties.
Lee (2006)	Ubiquitous accessibility, Situation-awareness, Fun.	The extent of the influence of the interactivity of mobile contents on ubiquitous services.	The interactivity of mobile services is applied to ubiquitous services.

Interactivity has a complex structure and is multi-dimensional. Moreover this research is viewing only a part of it thus this can be considered natural that definitions of research contents are different between various researchers. Burgoon et al. (2000) related that if involvement and mutuality as the quantitative experiences elucidating the characteristics of interactivity is high, reliability and attractiveness related to services would be enhanced to the encouragement of productivity enabling exchanging messages with better decision making and accurate understanding.

The most sophisticated definition of interactivity as a measurable variable was presented by Rafaeli (1998). He defined interactivity as, expressing in a given series of communication exchanges, the extent to which third messages are connected to the extent to which second messages exchanges are based on first messages. This viewpoint is significant in that it viewed interactivity from recursive perspectives rather than viewing it as sequences, timing, contents or a number of messages. Also, Dholakia et al. (2000) showed a similar viewpoint. They defined interactivity as the extent to which participants in communication processes control mutual discourses and exchange their roles.

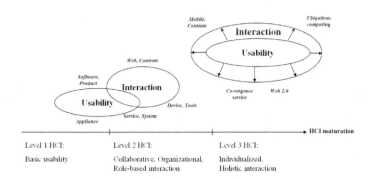

Figure 3. Changes in related researches with maturity in HCI area

(modified from Maxwell, 2001)

The researches related to interactions in Human Computer Interaction (HCI) have rapidly developed with the development of internet and reached at the current ubiquitous services along with researches into interactions of web sites and mobile services (Steitz et al., 2001). Maxwell (2001), who presented the maturity model in HCI research area, defined interactions as the most mature area in HCI area. Especially, he presented interactivity as an area transcending the research issue of basic usability (figure 3).

Level 1 indicates the stage of basic usability. The demands of usability have rapidly increased with the embedding of computers into machines in 1980s and major goals were about 'How can computers are made easily usable?'. It was researched centering on its major attributes including ease of use, ease of learning, error protection, graceful error recovery, and efficiency of performance. As the importance of usability emerged and was emphasized, an international standardization organization proposed Usability Maturity Model (UMM) in Human-Centered Design (HCD) guidelines (ISO TR 18529, 2000).

Level 2 was defined to be a stage related to collaboration, organization, and role-based interaction. Along with the spreading of distributed computers (Client-Server: C/S) and networks, the convergence of communication technologies and the expansion of devices mean researches into specified interactions with computers from sociological, organizational and cultural perspectives transcending the demands of basic usability.

Level 3 was defined from the viewpoint of individualized and holistic interaction. The holistic interactions with diverse products and/or services realized in ubiquitous (or invisible, embedded, interconnected, mobile) computer environments were defined as a concept to support the users adapting to new environments. Similar to holistic medicine, holistic interaction is positioning as a concept of accesses for those interaction designs such as productivity, performance, safety, teamwork and personal growth from the viewpoints of personal demands, goals and lifestyles (Beyer and Holtzblatt, 1997; Jenna and Geri, 2002).

Table 4. Major researches related to interactivity in HCI areas (modified from Kiousis, 2002; Lee, 2006)

Researcher	The definition and concept of interactivity
William et al. (1988)	In the course of communication between computer users, the extent to which communications between them are controlled and their roles are exchanged.
Heeter (1989)	Six aspects of interactivity between computers and humans: complexity in selection, levels of efforts, media responsiveness, ability to monitor media, ability to add information, inter-personal communication ability.
Steuer (1992)	The range in which computer users can revise the forms and contents of mediated environments at real times.
Hoffman and Novak (1996)	Human-Human Interactivity (HHI) is interactions between humans, and Media and Mechanical Interactivity (MMI) is interactions between humans and machines made to access to hypermedia contents.
Newhagen and Rafaeli (1996)	The communication ability to recollect and satisfy computers and objects themselves and to respond to the past.
Rogers (1996)	The ability of new communication systems giving the answers almost the same as those given by computer users participating in communications (computers are included mainly as the concept of composition).
Rafaeli (1998)	The exchange actions to be observed in user environments (the extent to which a message is related to the extension of previous message in communication exchanges). This requires exchangeable roles of communication for perfect communications while computers are used.
Yuping and Shrum (2002)	The extent to which computers and users, two or more communication parties can take actions toward the other on communication media or messages and the extent to which such influences are exerted simultaneously.
Fotin and Dholakia (2005)	The extent to which individuals or multiple users are permitted to communicate with each other as message senders and receivers in the state where searches for or accesses to real time or storage and transmission based information or order based information such as the contents, timing and orders of communications are under the control of final users (real time collaborations and multilateral interactivity were presented).

Intensive researches into interactivity were also emphasized in HCI areas such as Participatory Design (PD; Ehn, 1988) and interaction design (Preece et al., 2002). Thereby the areas such as mental-human processor, cognitive science perspectives, phenomenology and speech-act theory, ethnomethodology (ethnographic, anthropology), activity theory and semiotics, and dramatic theory were expanded into HCI areas initiating interactivity centered application and evaluation researches (Svanaes, 2000). Major research contents in HCI related areas are as table 4.

Also, the classification of interactivity components in HCI related areas can be defined as communication, connectivity, controllability, personalization, responsiveness, time, feedback, etc. (table 5).

As advanced researches into interactivity, characteristic-approach researches and perception-approach researches were executed (McMillan and Hwang, 2002). In their researches, users' involvements were analyzed, the extents of relations between services and users were presented and the inclusiveness of the factors that may control users was verified all utilizing interactivity. Table 6 shows the researches related to composite interactivity.

As quantitative experiences elucidating the characteristics of interactivity in HCI, Burgoon et al. (2000) proposed a framework consisting of 1) interaction involvement which is the extent to which computer users are cognitively, emotionally and behaviorally involved in interactions, 2) mutuality which is the extent to which computer users recognize and form relational sense of connection, mutual dependence, adjustment and understanding of others, 3) individualization which is the extent to which computer users feel that they know others' identities or personal information abundantly as well as in detail.

Table 5. Key components of interactivity (modified from Heeter, 1989; McMillan, 1999)

Component	Related researcher	Components used
Two-way communication	Neurman (1991)	Sender-receiver communication
	Zack (1993), Pavlik (1998), Yuping and Shrum (2002)	Two-way communication
	Hanssen et al. (1996)	Functional communication
	Bezjian-Avery et al. (1998)	Communication between consumers and manufacturers
	Ha and James (1998)	Mutual communication
	Heckel (1998), Cho and Leckenby (1999)	Exchange, Mutual exchange
	Carey (1989), Lieb (1998)	Human to human communication
	McMillan (2002)	Communication direction
Connectivity	Ku (1992)	Communication connectivity
	Ha and James (1998)	Connectivity
Controllability	Steuer (1992)	Real time participation
	Bezjian-Avery et al. (1998)	User control
	Wu (2000)	Crossed user control
	Coyle and Thorson (2001)	Perceived controllability
	McMillan (2002)	Control
Personalization	Lieb (1998), Dholakia et al. (2000), Wu (2000)	Personalization
Responsiveness	Miles (1992), Hanssen et al. (1996), Rafaeli (1998)	Responsiveness
	Ha and James (1998)	Response, responsiveness to users
	Heeter (1989, 2000), Wu (1999, 2000)	Perceived responsiveness
Time	Novak et al. (2000)	Time required for interactions
	McMillan (2000)	Time sensitivity
	Coyle and Thorson (2001)	Speed
	McMillan (2002)	Time
Searchableness	Hoffman and Novak (1996)	Search
	Wu (1999)	Search or navigation
	Haubl and Trift (2000)	Quantity and quality of information search
Feedback	Anderson (1986)	Real time feedback
	Ku (1992), Straubhaar and LaRose (1996)	Immediateness of feedback

Table 6. Research related to composite interactivity definition (modified from McMillan and Hwang, 2002; Lee, 2003)

Researcher	Description of interactivity
Heeter (1989)	Multi-dimensional concept; complexity of choice available, efforts, responsiveness to the user, monitoring information use, ease of adding information, inter-personal communication.
Zack (1993)	The simultaneous and continuous exchange of information, the use of multiple non-verbal cues, the potentially spontaneous, unpredictable, and emergent progression of remarks, the ability to interrupt or preempt, mutuality, patterns of turn-taking, and the use of adjacency pairs.
Hanssen et al. (1996)	Equality (containing aspects such as participants, mutual activity, role exchange, control), responsiveness (mutual discourse, nature of feedback, response time), functional communicative environment (bandwidth, transparency, social presence, artificial intelligence).
Lieb (1998)	The first is a kind of personalization and the second type is community building.
Coyle and Thorson (2001)	A web site that is described as interactive should have good mapping, quick transitions between a user's input and resulting actions, and a range of ways to manipulate the content.
McMillan (2002)	Identifies four types of interactivity based on intersection of user control and direction of communication; monologue, feedback, responsive dialogue, and mutual discourse.

In most cases, major factors of interactions involve considerable amounts of overlapping concepts. Accordingly, researches into perception based interactivity, Measures of Perceived Interactivity (MPI), a measuring tool for perceived interactivity was developed and MPI made evaluations involving those constituents such as real time conversation, no-delay, engaging, etc. (McMillan and Hwang, 2002). Table 7 shows the contents of the researches utilizing MPI.

Table 7. Researches into the factors affecting perceived interactivity (modified from McMillan 2000; McMillan and Hwang, 2002)

Researcher	Independent variable	Dependent variable	Research result
Wu (1999)	Searchableness, Responsiveness.	Attitude.	Perceived interactivity increases web site attitudes.
Jee and Lee (2002)	Desire for cognition, Product involvement, Product specialty, Skillfulness, Sense of challenge, Experience.	Perceived interactivity, Attitudes, Intention.	Desire for cognition and involvement as personal factors and skillfulness, sense of challenge and web surfing experiences as online factors precede interactivity.
Sohn, Leckenby and Jee (2003)	Expected interactivity, Market mastery.	Perceived interactivity.	Expected interactivity and marketability exert influences on perceived interactivity depending on the height of the interactivity of a site.
Sohn and Lee (2005)	Desire for cognition, Frequency, Network intensity, Time.	Perceived interactivity (Perceived controllability, Perceived responsiveness, Interaction effect).	Desire for cognition, frequency, network, use time etc. as social, psychological factors exert influences on the dimension of perceived interactivity.
Wu (2005)	Actual interactivity.	Interactivity perceived as a parameter, Attitude.	Actual interactivity influences attitudes toward web sites through the mediation of perceived interactivity.

If the researches are related to interactivity in HCI areas, it can be seen that the factors related to communication direction, user controllability and time are important.

1) As for direction of communication, bi-directional communication was presented as a key factor and defined as the level of mutual responses.

2) User controllability means the interactivity enabling users to freely select the contents, formats, orders and more of information as their needs. Computer related user researches mainly conducted into user interfaces and input devices, navigation tools, user options, system activities, etc. (Hoffman and Novak, 1996).

3) Since time factor is affected by the speed of message transmissions and processing

done by individuals, response speed has been highlighted as a key factor for both of users and service systems.

(2) Researches into interactivity in ubiquitous environments

The interaction researches related to mobile services before ubiquitous services were executed on inter-personal communications made through traditional voice calls, and message transmissions with letters, sounds or images and user-machine interactions made between mobile contents and users such as browsing, downloads, streaming and push services. In the mobile environments underlying ubiquitous networks, close and sustained interactions among companies, users and contents providers will be increased anytime anywhere without temporal and spatial restrictions (Kalakota and Robinson, 2002).

In online and mobile interactivity research scopes, limitations exist in understanding new characteristics of interactivity such as ubiquitous interaction, continued interaction and context-awareness. Consequently, for the understanding of the interactivity arising in ubiquitous environments, the interactivity research perspectives in existing online and/or mobile environments need to be expended (Kannan et al., 2001; Lee, 2005).

Also, since 1998, researches into the evaluations of UCD based ubiquitous computing applications have been steadily executed in Ubiquitous Computing associate (hereinafter, UbiComp) workshops (Mallon and Webb, 2000; UbiComp01, 2001; Barnard et al., 2002; UbiComp02, 2002). But they are on the level where the evaluations centered on level 1, 'basic usability' in which HCI maturity were simply reformed to become suitable to ubiquitous environments, thus it should be too much if one argues the evaluations 'became ubiquitous' in a true meaning (UbiComp02, 2002).

Yadav and Varadarajan (2005) hammered out diverse evaluation factors through interactivity researches in the environments where computer media mediate in e-

Marketplaces. The conceptual factors for evaluations were classified into purchasers, sellers, messages and devices, and operational measurement variables for each of them were proposed (table 8). The proposed factors carry a great significance in that they presented direct measures for service quality improvements by presenting concrete evaluation methods for each of the media composing e-Marketplaces.

In the research of Olson and Olson (2000), the concept of perceived interactivity linked to ubiquitous service characteristics was concretized and the relations were verified through empirical studies. Also, Reichl and Hammer (2004) presented the methods to evaluate interactivity centering on mobile devices. The interactivity in mobile was classified into a technology structure, communication environments and user perceptions for build up the model.

Figure 4 shows the evaluation structure for the proposed mobile interactivity. But, in their researches, interactivity evaluations were analyzed centering on quantitative evaluations (time, speed, error rate, etc.). Thus there were limitations in analyzing user satisfaction or preference through interactions.

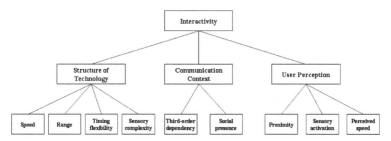

Figure 4. The structure of the interactivity for mobile service evaluations

(Reichl and Hammer, 2004)

Table 8. Examples of the characteristics of computer-mediated interactivity (modified from Yadav and Varadarajan, 2005)

Subject of conceptualization	Content	Operational variable
e-Marketplace purchaser device	· Response time: responding speed of interface (computerized shopping interface) · Degree of correspondence: degree of response to requests for information and answers	· Response time · Response contingency
	· Level of control: the level of control where users can deal with information to enable fast purchases, quality for product selection is improved	· Level of control
e-Marketplace seller device	· Control: users understand device characteristics and devices help in information managing ability	· Level of control
e-Marketplace buyer-seller message	· Both message senders and receiver: participants are senders and receivers of messages and bidirectional communications are required from many factors	· Directionality of communication · Interchangeability
	· Precision: seller messages should be accurately delivered to buyers	· Massage addressability
	· Contingency (response depends on prior exchange) and Synchronicity (speed of response): diverse measures should be presented on fast response levels	· Degree of contingency · Frequency · Sensory involvement · Synchronicity
User device, message	· Sense of mutual interdependence: personal perceptions of interactivity help users use actively and friendly	· Interaction involvement · Mutuality · Individuation
	· Communication: bi-directional communications improve interactivity, contingency, transformation, participation, and synchronicity · Technical capability: technical importance to improve communications	· Direction of communication · Time flexibility · Complexity · Effort · Information updating
	· Technologies: diversity of functions, diversity of selection, the technology that can be personalized, consistency enabling uses in different situations, generality enabling applications to diverse users	· Selectivity · Modifiability · Multi-sensory experience

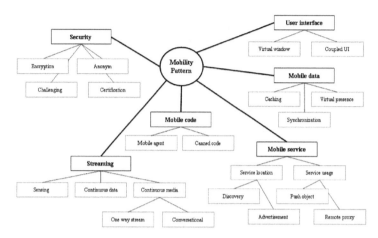

Figure 5. Mobile pattern hierarchy (modified from Roth, 2002)

Downes and McMillan (2000) proposed a five-dimensional interactivity evaluation framework. The framework was proposed with direction of communication, timing flexibility, sense of place, level of control, and responsiveness revealed the direction of communication and timing flexibility as the most important key factors.

The evaluation research related to mobility among ubiquitous service characteristics was concretized by Roth (2002). Through mobile interaction pattern analyses, the interactivity characteristics of mobility in mobile devices were approached from the aspects of mobile services, UI, data, security, streaming (figure 5), and nine mobility patterns for evolved interactivity were proposed.

As shown in figure 6, implicit interaction is especially required in ubiquitous service environments and this is the most clearly distinguished difference from digital service environments. In digital environments, computers are exposed externally, and the works to be done by users through computers are relatively obvious.

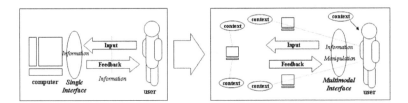

Figure 6. Implicit interactions between users and interfaces in ubiquitous environments (modified from Gopalakrishnan, 2001; Lee, 2003; Schmidt, 2003-a)

Thus there are explicit interactions where interfaces react only to direct inputs from users. However, in ubiquitous environments, interfaces hiding in backgrounds, there are the characteristics of implicit interactions where users are provided with services in their lives without perception through diverse input and/or output devices (multimodality) (Christensen and Olson, 2002; Mankoff et al., 2003; Peter et al., 2003). For the detailed examples, see Appendix A.

2.2 Approaches to ubiquitous service evaluations

2.2.1 Approach to User-Centered Design (UCD)

The UCD approaches to the evaluations of ubiquitous computing application can be applied in three methods; field survey, rapid prototyping and scenario development. The researches into ubiquitous service designing and evaluation utilizing UCD are not being applied in the level applicable to practices like in online and/or mobile service area (Stephanidis and Savidis, 2003; Carolis et al., 2004; Nakagawa et al., 2004; Evans and Gibbons, 2006; Thatcher, 2006). Among the researches related to ubiquitous service evaluations, most researches attempted ubiquitous services and their evaluations in the state where ubiquitous computing environments were not yet activated. Especially the researches related to evaluation scopes were actively executed in computing related performance evaluation studies and the researches from HCI perspective were executed in a low range on the level of laboratory experiments (Sweeney, 1993; Burnett and Rainsford, 2001; Arnstein et al., 2006; Kwon et al., 2006).

Scholtz et al. (2002) attempted to classify complex socio-technical systems structures centering on UCD for evaluations. The characteristic of this research is that eleven factors including 1) large problem spaces, 2) social, 3) heterogeneous perspectives, 4) distributed, 5) dynamic, 6) potentially high hazards, 7) many coupled subsystems, 8) significant use of automation, 9) uncertain data, 10) mediated interaction via computers, and 11) disturbances were presented as evaluation criteria for ubiquitous service related national tasks.

The approaches to evaluations utilizing UCD applied the evaluation concepts for the realization of the service environments where services and information can be obtained anytime anywhere without interference (Tracy, 2001; Gay and Hembrooke, 2004). The conceptual components to understand individuals' environments and intentions were composed of personal facial expressions, speech, gestures, attention (e.g.: who is present, who is speaking and about what), and there significance lies in the fact that they proposed the systems where social dynamics can be supported or monitored. In their research, the methodology of the UCD for the services and systems supporting co-located communication and collaboration was presented, and traditional HCI methods were integrated with the methods used in collaborative works for the evaluation of ubiquitous services. The UCD methodology proposed as Computers in the Human Interaction Loop (CHIL) project aimed at combining task oriented approaches and social dynamics approaches and CHIL project aimed at the realization of the environment for the evaluation of the large scaled service systems focused on the interactions with other user and computers.

In UbiComp workshops (UbiComp01, 2001; UbiComp02, 2002), the researches related to the development of evaluation methodologies for ubiquitous computing were steadily executed and the framework that composed the evaluation factors utilizing UCD with universality, utility, usability, and ubiquity was presented (table 9).

The researches into the integration and concretization of the factors of conceptual evaluation methods and areas divisions were executed. The researches to define ubiquitous service architectures and the evaluation factors of each component were attempted (Garlan et al., 2002; Eleni and Achilles, 2005).

Table 9. Evaluation methodologies for ubiquitous service computing (UbiComp01, 2001)

Component	Definition/Metric	Challenge for evaluation/Tools needed
Universality	For who and applicable domain · Personal information · Training	· New use cases: workload, metrics, and stress points aren't identified · No reference points · Recommendations for metrics for various use cases · New prototyping tools
Utility	Benefit to users · Inferencing	· Frame problem: what data do we need to capture, how that data can be captured · Evaluation technologies for system in use · Multimodal I/O · Simulations for devices · Personal event capture
Usability	Effort per utility unit · Configuration · Predictability · Distraction · Mixed initiative	· How do we capture users' intent? · Finer grain attention analysis · New coding techniques for situational data captured (parallel interactions with other devices, situational information, etc.) · Multiple streams of data need to be visualized
Ubiquity	Points of delivery in physical world (where) and when · Graceful degradation · Trust	· Larger set of degraded operating modes · Simulations for degraded conditions · Ability to simulate: degraded system modes · Separate bus: personal event capturer, rotating buffer

Especially, Scholtz and Consolvo (2004) pointed out the limitations of existing researches, with their low utility and presented 'the framework of Ubiquitous computing Evaluation Areas (UEAs)' composed of nine evaluation areas. The proposed framework carries its significance in that it is a ubiquitous service evaluation framework applied to practices (table 10).

Also, Arnstein et al. (2006) classified ubiquitous service evaluation ranges into 'system manager: configuration', 'user: robustness', and 'developer: extensibility', and presented factors so that the evaluations reflecting each characteristics can be made.

National Center of excellence for Ubiquitous Computing and Networking (CUCN) presented a keyword centered evaluation method and defined its standard items as three keywords; situation sensing (decision), autonomic computing, and self-growing intelligence engine, and relocated sub-items to measure evaluation items (table 11).

Table 10. UEAs: framework of Ubiquitous computing Evaluation Areas (Scholtz and Consolvo, 2004)

Ubiquitous evaluation areas	Metrics component
Attention	Focus, Overhead.
Adoption	Rate, Value, Cost, Availability, Flexibility.
Trust	Privacy, Awareness, Control.
Conceptual model	Predictability of application behavior, Awareness of application capabilities, Vocabulary-awareness.
Interaction	Effectiveness, Efficiency, User satisfaction, Distraction, Interaction transparency, Scalability, Collaborative interaction.
Invisibility	Intelligibility, Control, Accuracy, Customization.
Impact and side effects	Utility, Behavior changes, Social acceptance, Environment change.
Appeal	Fun, Aesthetics, Status.
Application robustness	Robustness, Performance speed, Volatility.

Table 11. Definition of 3 keywords evaluation method (CUCN, 2005)

3 keywords	Definition/Explanation
Situation sensing (decision)	To sense diverse situations and infer user intentions in order to solve problems.
Autonomic computing	To be entrusted with authority from users in order to achieve goals through autonomic reorganization and treatments.
Self-growing intelligence engine	User purpose oriented self-growing intelligence engine.

Three keywords evaluation was proposed for the evaluation of ubiquitous community service that would compose voluntary communities of intelligent entities where users coexist with objects and define shared roles among members in order to provide optimum services for each situation (CUCN, 2005).

In the research of Jo et al. (2006), it was argued that ubiquitous service evaluations depend on how much the abilities embedded in ubiquitous computing technologies are reflected. A research was executed on how these abilities influence ubiquitous service quality.

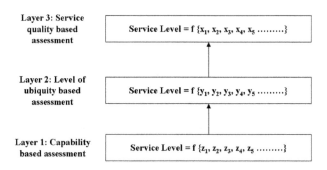

Layer 3: Service quality based assessment   Service Level = f $\{x_1, x_2, x_3, x_4, x_5 \ldots\ldots\}$

Layer 2: Level of ubiquity based assessment   Service Level = f $\{y_1, y_2, y_3, y_4, y_5 \ldots\ldots\}$

Layer 1: Capability based assessment   Service Level = f $\{z_1, z_2, z_3, z_4, z_5 \ldots\ldots\}$

Figure 7. 3 levels model for service level evaluation (Jo et al., 2006)

As per figure 7, ubiquitous service levels were defined in three levels (capability, ubiquity, service quality) and the regression method was utilized through evaluations by each levels.

The researches into the evaluations of specialized ubiquitous services were actively executed in education service (u-Learning) where traditional computer-supported learning evaluation methodologies were utilized to present the framework for the evaluation of one-to-one (1:1) customized service between students and ubiquitous services (Zucker et al., 2006).

Also, a research with affective engineering (Kansei engineering) based approach was attempted for ubiquitous computing service evaluations and Riekki et al. (2004) executed emotion evaluations on 'Calmness' of ubiquitous services. In order to analyze the characteristic where the methods to provide services do not annoy and obtrusive users but services are provided quietly only when required by users, calm interactions and calm timing were proposed as frameworks (figure 8), and levels were measured by services to extract emotion models.

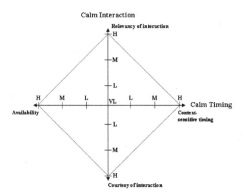

Figure 8. Framework to evaluate the extent of Calmness (Riekki et al., 2004)

(VL: Very Low, L: Low, M: Medium, H: High)

Kim (2005)'s research indicated infra-architecture for model embodiment of context-awareness for an affective evaluation on ubiquitous service. The existing context-awareness system identifies the object from the states of things occurred and focuses mainly on cognition of them caused by the object.

However, in order to make a proposal algorithm which can support potential required service and technique architecture, he suggested a make-up and a system of multimodal input device on sensing system for data input available in face recognition, gesture, a voice, a temperature, humidity, the weather and so on.

The study of Ryu et al. (2006) proposed ISO 9241-9 and -11 (1998) for software evaluation basis on a quality and Ubiquitous Computing Service Framework (UCSF; figure 9).

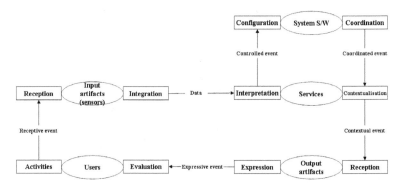

Figure 9. Framework on ubiquitous service system evaluation (Ryu et al., 2006)

The framework composed of five entities (users, input artifacts, services, system software, output artifacts) and ten functions (activities, reception, integration, interpretation, configuration, coordination contextualization, reception, expression, evaluation) suggested a evaluation basis in detail into composed factor for ISO-9241, and was composed of being focused on a evaluation on quality and capacity .

To apply for specialized ubiquitous service industry, a framework on integrated New Product Design (iNPD) available in a plan and a evaluation in service product toward personnel was proposed. The iNPD framework stressed process suited to user experience (Cagan and Vogal, 2002; figure 10). Experience-centered evaluation method defined as User-eXperience Design (UXD) has been used for a evaluation method such as diary-study. A simple method for ubiquitous service evaluation has been offered as well (Mankoff and Carter, 2005).

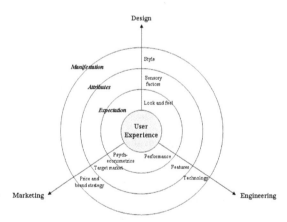

Figure 10. User-Centered Design (UCD) and integrated New Product Development (iNPD): the user's expectation sets up attributes that are manifested through the disciplines (Cagan and Vogel, 2002)

Table 12. Human-centered service evaluation framework: TELU (Jo et al., 2006)

General scenario (5W1H)	Ubiquitous service scenario
What	Event: events happening in ubiquitous service.
When	Time: time when ubiquitous service is supplied.
Why	Need: a function that a customer is requiring on ubiquitous service.
Who	User: a received person from ubiquitous service.
Where	Location: a special concept where each event is occurred on ubiquitous service.
How	Service: ubiquitous service supplied for a user.

Lee (2006) suggested an article on human-centered service evaluation method, which was for development of a framework to select human-centered service area in terms of construction for ubiquitous city (u-City). Evaluated factor of suggested framework was defined as TELU (Time, Event, Location, and User), and each factor was done to evaluate in being matched with conditions of 5W1H (table 12).

A method on human-centered service area in the center of a special feature on TELU is defined as a start-up point for human requirement, not a technology, and the meaning is to determine and select which service will be needed at first in terms of a user. A new process was offered as a user-centered evaluation on ubiquitous service development.

Main framework on ubiquitous service evaluation is as follows (table 13). For the detailed examples, see Appendix B.

2.2.2 Approaches to psychometric theory

As one of user evaluation methods in ubiquitous service, a method related to a psychological evaluation was attempted for user satisfaction on ubiquitous service used in psychometrics. The purpose of psychometrics (or measuring psychology) is defined as a method for an establishment of quality system in mental and/or psychological measure (Nunnally and Bernstein, 1994). Namely, it is defined as one of psychology measures dealt with evaluated factors to estimate psychological measures, and currently include an evaluation on psychological contents as well as multiple activities in daily life (Edenborough, 1998). Cognitive and psychological measurement in a variety of types is offered more, and it is used in science and/or engineering area such as cognitive science, HCI, human factors (ergonomics) and so on, which is used as a fundamental theory of an investigation method like affective evaluation, satisfactory evaluation, preferred investigation, etc. (Wu and Wang, 2007).

Table 13. Major ubiquitous service evaluation frameworks utilizing UCD

Methodology/Researcher	Evaluation key factors	Main architecture
4U: UbiComp (2001; 2002)	University, Utility, Usability, Ubiquity.	The first proposal on a theoretical ubiquitous service evaluation method.
UEAs: Scholtz and Consolvo (2004)	Attention, Adoption, Trust, Conceptual model, Interaction, Invisibility, Impact and side effects, Appeal, Application robustness.	Development for evaluation method on business practice case (IBM).
Calmness: Riekki et al. (2004)	Relevancy of interaction, Context-sensitivity timing, Courtesy of interaction, Availability.	An evaluated technique used on affective (Kansei) engineering.
3 keywords approach: CUCN (2005)	Situation sensing, Automatic computing, Self-growing intelligence engine.	A technique on an efficiency evaluation per service system.
TELU: Lee (2006)	Time, Event, Location, User.	Human-centered evaluation technique.
5 entities, 10 functions: Ryu et al. (2006)	Activities, Evaluation, Reception, Integration, Expression, Functionality, Service quality, Contextualization, Service and privacy, Configuration, Coordination.	A user, service, system and evaluated technique per composed factors (ISO 9241).
3 levels approach: Jo et al. (2006)	Capability, Ubiquity, Service quality.	An evaluation on quality level used in user satisfaction (regression method).
Intel's evaluation scope: Arnstein et al. (2006)	Configurability and the system administrator, Robustness and the user, Extensibility and the developer.	Contents of business practice considered in terms of a service system, a user, and a developer.

Table 14. Major purposes of psychometrics (modified from Nunnally and Bernstein, 1994; Lewis, 2002)

Analysis Process	Definition	Analysis/Estimation method
Reliability	Can measurement be reliable?	·Coefficient alpha (0: no, 1: perfect) ·Accepted in case of value amounting to at least more than .8
Validity	Is it available for given trusted measurement?	·Pearson correlation coefficient ($-1 \leq r \leq 1$) ·The higher the absolute value is, the more it is accepted
Sensitivity	Is measurement sensitive to experimental operation (pursuit for difference) suitably?	·ANOVA ·GLM

Especially, to measure not a physical object, in case of parameter factor or temporary substance, the main goal for investigation is on how exact it is extracted from measurement of user concept. Psychometrics on multiple approachable features in method of application and forms of expression includes things related with reliability, validity, and sensitivity analysis (table 14).

In terms of psychometrics, factor analysis and a scale step needed to extract main factor have begun to use seven point scales making a use of experimental result by a drop of reliability from seven steps. Loading (additional) value per variable avoids multicollinearity and designates equal weight to consider advantage on analysis of the measured result. An inquiry uses more unipolar (designated as one to seven both of all named center as four points) rather than bipolar (designated into both a negative number and a positive one focused on '0' from center) and brings out reliable results by using an antonym rather than a negative word (Lewis, 1995). Also, in psychometrics, it tends to prefer Classical Test Theory (CTT) to Item Response Theory (IRT), which means IRT needs to investigate a lot of specimen and cannot establish a general model so that all of multiple information can be explained, hence it has a difficult meaning due to a complicated result by means of method to support information per individual ability by extracting user individual (reflection of discriminated feature on capacity, gender, and so on) questions (Parasuraman and Zeithaml, 1994).

Main differences between formative and summative evaluation generally used in engineering in sorts of evaluation suggested in psychometrics are as follows. Formative evaluation is an evaluation method for supporting information for a designer and a developer who design services and applications with feedback from a user in preliminary version. Summative evaluation cannot demonstrate convenience for use in system or determine the capacity of a product; it is used to supply information for an outsider or a user on service or the capacity of an application. Therefore, application of psychometrics in ubiquitous service evaluation is focused on the development of a summative evaluation framework by a use of CTT technique. Evaluation techniques used in psychometrics were applied a lot in online service, mobile service, or framework development for evaluation in everyday product use, the development of evaluation index (Igbaria et al., 1997).

Kim et al. (2006), in his study, makes a use of structured equation model in order to develop evaluation index on utility of ubiquitous service, and the evaluation index on utility of ubiquitous service. It was offered four factors; ubiquitous characteristics, usability (ease of use), performance or capacity, and reliability or safety.

Scholtz (2001; 2006) made a use of bibliometrics (to apply mathematical or statistical method in return for expressed knowledge), which evaluation factors on large scale service system (Human Information Interaction: HII) through mutual relation between an user and information just like ubiquitous service could be suggested into performance or algorithm evaluations, usability or interaction evaluation, overall impact or process evaluation and so on, which are done by three varieties. Framework for HII service system evaluation in detail needed to define and evaluate relation with usability, performance, and utility metrics (figure 11).

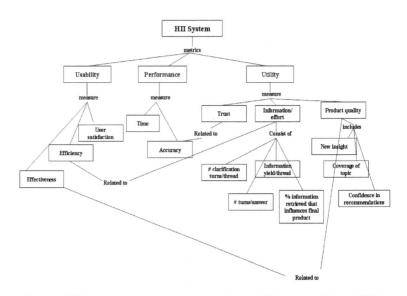

Figure 11. HII service evaluation framework utilizing bibliometrics (Scholtz, 2006)

Concrete evaluation index is as follows (table 15).

Table 15. Examples: HII service system metrics (Scholtz, 2006)

Evaluation index	Metric
Analysis time	Total consuming time, Time for data collection, Loading time on results, Task switching time, Task number a user is using at the same time.
Data coverage	Total knowledge % supplied by system, % for related results are arranged.
Analysis process	Inter-operability of devices, Consistency for usage among devices, Flexibility of devices by a difference in terms of individual and environment.
Analysis facilitation	Software usability, User satisfaction, Level on declined effort.
Product quality	User satisfaction on product, Expert decision on service offer.

Mack et al. (2004) suggested the psychometrics method in detail on how each user's experience could affect service capacity and satisfaction in return of a large scale service system. In returns of Terrorism Information Awareness (TIA) service system, it would be evaluated in terms of cognitive, operational, and technical. As a result, through modeling technique in psychometrics, five threads (process group) were offered (structured discovery; link and group understanding; decision-making with corporate memory; collaborative problem solving; context-aware visualization), operational environment (operational context-mission, goals, resources) and also additional evaluation factor was defined in equation (1).

$$Y(\text{system behavior}) = f_n \{X_1(\text{configuration of interators}), \tag{1}$$
$$X_2(\text{interactors' individual capabilities}),$$
$$X_3(\text{requirements that must be met to use those capabilities}),$$
$$X_4(\text{regime of dynamic control and coordination of the interactors})\}$$

2.2.3 Approaches to Usability Evaluation Methodology (UEM)

Usability feature accounted in approach of the UCD technique, approach method in a point of view means a property used in special environment with users' purpose in detail. User problem is to handle the interaction between product (and/or system) and user caused when user handles a special device. Feature learnability on product, efficiency, memorability, error tolerance, satisfaction, etc. in usability has been studied significantly (Nielsen, 1993). Especially, in terms of usability engineering, heuristic evaluation for usability evaluation has been developed so far (Nielsen, 1994; Bonnie, 1996).

Regulations on usability evaluation methodology offered in International Standard Organization (ISO) are as follows (table 16).

Table 16. International Standard Organization (ISO) related to usability (modified from Scholtz, 2003)

ISO Standard	Contents
ISO/IEC* 9126 (parts 1-4), ISO 20282, ISO 9241-11/29	Software engineering, usability guidelines, quality in use, internal and external metrics, product quality, task requirements.
ISO 9241 (parts 3-17)	Ergonomics requirements for Visual Display Terminals (VDT).
ISO 13406	Ergonomics requirements for flat panel displays.
ISO/IEC 18019	User software documentation process.
ISO/IEC 15910	Design guidelines for user documentation.
ISO 15939	Software engineering: Software measurement process.
ISO 13407	Human-centered design process and usability.
ISO TR** 16982	Ergonomics of human-system interaction: Usability methods supporting human-centered design.
ISO TR 18529	Ergonomics of human-system interaction: Human-centered lifecycle process descriptions.
ISO/IEC 10741-1	Dialogue interaction.
ISO/IEC 11581	Icon symbols and foundations.
ISO 14915	Software ergonomics for multimedia user interfaces.
ISO/IEC 14754	Pen-based interfaces.
ISO/IEC 18021	User interfaces for mobile tools.
ISO/IEC 10075-1	Ergonomics principles for mental workload.
ISO/IEC 25000	Software engineering: Software product Quality Requirements and Evaluation (SQuaRE): Guide to SQuaRE.

*: IEC: International Electrotechnical Commission, **: TR: Technical Report

Feature on usability has been defined and emphasized into other terms and features in terms of study related with HCI. Nielsen (1993) defined components on usability as efficiency, learning ability, memory capacity, satisfaction, etc. and similarly, the study of Constantine and Lockwood (1999) indicated factors in terms of efficiency, learning ability, and reliability. They defined components on usability in similar words from a variety of researches, however in ISO 9241-11 (1998), they indicated components standard on usability in terms of effectiveness, efficiency, and user satisfaction (table 17).

Table 17. Major ranges of usability components

Researcher	Component/Scope				
Shackel (1991)	Effectiveness: speed	Learnability: time to learn	Learnability: retention	Effectiveness: errors	Attitude
Nielsen (1993)	Efficiency of use	Ease of learning	Memorability	Errors/safety	Satisfaction
ISO 9241-11 (1998)	Efficiency	-	-	Effectiveness	Satisfaction
Schneiderman (1998)	Speed	Time to learn	Over time	Error rate	Satisfaction
Contantine and Lockwood (1999)	Efficiency in use	Learnability	Rememberability	Reliability in use	User satisfaction
Preece et al. (2002)	Throughput	Ease of learning	-	-	Attitude

The researches in user evaluation methods utilized for UCD have been presented from various viewpoints for thirty years (Scholtz and Consolvo, 2004; Seffah et al., 2006). Especially, the researches in usability evaluation methodologies have been intensively executed from the 1980s centering on the development of the questionnaires using psychometrics (figure 12; table 19).

Table 18. Usability test and evaluation guidelines (Sears, 2003; Kleef et al., 2005)

Evaluation concept	Characteristics	Technique/Method
User-based evaluations	User participation	Questionnaire, Observing users, Empirical usability testing.
Inspection-based evaluations	Usability Inspection Method (UIM)	Heuristic evaluation, Guideline based methods, Cognitive walk-through, Hybrid method: Heuristic walkthrough.
Model-based evaluations	Using a model: predicted usability measures by calculation or simulation	Task network models, Cognitive architecture models, GOMS models.

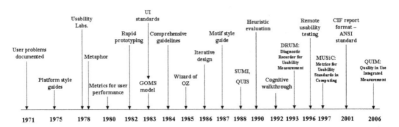

Figure 12. User evaluation methods developed after 1971
(modified from Scholtz and Consolvo, 2004; Seffah et al., 2006)

In guidelines shown in ISO, especially, an evaluation technique (considered technological, physical, social feature) considering user characteristics and context of use was introduced (ISO 9241-11, 1998), the lack of attributes for user performance evaluation in interactive systems and/or service such as mobile application was yet pointed out as a disadvantage (Seffah et al., 2006). In current researches, Sears (2003) suggested index standard related to usability test, user testing and evaluation in table 18.

Major contents of user-centered usability evaluation methodologies (SUMI, SUS, QUIS, PSSUQ, QUIM) are as follows.

(1) SUMI: Software Usability Measurement Inventory (Kirakowski and Corett, 1993)

SUMI is a checklist and a survey method proposed by Human Factor Research Group, University College Cork (HFRG). The researches of HFRG began with the development of Computer User Satisfaction Inventory (CUSI) to complete SUMI, and the proposed method consists of fifty questionnaires evaluating user satisfaction on the five aspects of likability, efficiency, helpfulness, control and learnability. This method does not only refer to standard database supporting evaluations but also provides software for scoring.

Individuals' evaluation scores are linked to the reference model of SUMI to help judgments of overall levels of usability. SUMI is being proposed as a usability evaluation method most frequently used together with QUIS (Preece et al., 2002).

(2) SUS: System Usability Scale (Brooke, 1996)

Composed of ten questionnaires, SUS was developed to evaluate overall satisfaction of software products. The development was intended to enable the testing of users' subjectivities through methods to compare between software products and scoring through easy tests (minimum questionnaires). The questionnaires utilizing five points Likert scale expressed composite evaluations of the usability of systems, products or research outcomes. Major evaluation parameters were defined to be ease of learning, consistency, integration and ease of use, and confidence in using the system.

Table 19. User-centered usability evaluation methodologies (20 years: 1988~2007)

Year	Method	Description	Researcher
1988	QUIS-1	Questionnaire for User Interaction Satisfaction-1	Chin, Diehl and Norman
1988	CUSI	Computer User Satisfaction Inventory	Kirakowski and Corett
1989	SUMS	System Usability MetricS	Suzanne Henry (IBM)
1992	PSSUQ-1	Post Study System Usability Questionnaire	Lewis (IBM)
	CSUQ	Computer System Usability Questionnaire	
1993	SUMI	Software Usability Measurement Inventory	HFRG (Human Factors Research Group)
1995	MUMMS	Measuring the Usability of Multi-Media Software	HFRG (Human Factors Research Group)
1996	SUS	System Usability Scale	Brooke
1997	WAMMI	Website Analysis and MeasureMent Inventory	HFRG (Human Factors Research Group)
1998	QUIS-2	Questionnaire for User Interaction Satisfaction-2	Shneiderman
2002	PSSUQ-2	Post Study System Usability Questionnaire-2	Lewis (IBM)
2006	QUIM	Quality in Use Integrated Measurement	Seffah et al.

(3) QUIS: Questionnaire for User Interaction Satisfaction (Schneiderman, 1998)

Though it is somewhat similar to SUMI, QUIS was developed in order to evaluate user attitudes toward eleven factors (eleven factors: screen factors, terminology and system feedbacks, learning factors, system capabilities, technical manuals, on-line tutorials, multimedia, voice recognition, virtual environments, internet access, and software installation). By measuring overall user satisfactions in the proposed factors utilizing nine points Likert scale, it made an important contribution as an evaluation checklist for experts (QUIS, 2003; Akilli, 2005).

(4) PSSUQ: Post Study System Usability Questionnaire (Lewis, 2002)

An evaluation index dividing usability into three stepwise differentiated groups (ASQ, PSSUQ, and CSUQ) was developed and proposed. Also, PPSUQ has been utilized for the evaluation of the usability of IBM products contributing to the enhancement of product satisfactions. The proposed evaluation factors are largely three; all consisting of seven points Likert scales. By evaluating eighteen items separately with sub-indices given to each of the evaluation factors consisting system usefulness, information quality and interface quality, it was utilized for practical researches on finding the usability factors that influence productivity (table 20).

Table 20. Questionnaire groups by usability stages proposed by Lewis (1999; 2002)

Phase	Survey group	Example
After a task in usability test	ASQ (After Scenario Questionnaire)	Interaction response rate, suitability of information-support.
Post-study evaluation of usability test	PSSUQ (Post Study System Usability Questionnaire)	User experience level, explain-support of specific task.
Field studies	CSUQ (Computer System Usability Questionnaire)	Usability evaluation system level in field-support.

(5) QUIM: Quality in Use Integrated Measurement (Seffah et al., 2006)

Since 2000, the researches attempting to integrate models mentioned above into one along with the incorporation of ISO guidelines were executed. QUIM was proposed in order to structure diverse angles of sight and explain them with usability evaluation models. QUIM was composed of ten factors, twenty-six measurable criteria and a hundred and twenty-seven specific metrics. By embodying an automation tool called QUIM Editor, a system where real time evaluations may be feedbacked and shared was proposed (http://rana.cs.concordia.ca/odusim). This was developed in order to complement existing evaluation methodologies where consistencies between evaluators were low due to their high dependencies on experiences. It systemized many evaluation factors (table 21) and proposed evaluation methods, but it has not yet been generalized because it cannot present differences in importance and priorities between evaluation factors, and also because of its complexity and difficulty.

The researches into user-centered usability evaluation methodologies have the advantages. First, it can be utilized for the evaluations of user satisfactions utilizing standardized questionnaires. Second, it can provide filed staffs such as designers in product development with the checklist that can be reviewed quickly. Also, the significance of it lies in the fact that the development of factors that can be applied to diverse industries is continuously required, as the usability evaluation methods that were limited to certain industries or products develop into the areas of the products and services related to multimedia and mobile (Myers et al., 2000).

As for the research on Usability Maturity Model (UMM; Earthy, 1998-a; 1998-b) proposed as an advanced model for usability maturity, and the expanded research was executed in connection with Usability Capability Assessment (UCA).

Table 21. Relations between factors and criteria in QUIM (Seffah et al., 2006)

Factor / Criteria	Efficiency	Effectiveness	Satisfaction	Productivity	Learnability	Trustfulness	Accessibility	Universality
Time behavior	+			+				
Resource utilization	+			+				
Attractiveness			+					+
Likeability			+					
Flexibility		+	+				+	+
Minimal action	+		+		+		+	
Minimal memory load	+		+		+		+	+
Operability	+		+			+	+	
User guidance			+		+		+	+
Consistency		+			+		+	+
Self-descriptiveness					+	+	+	+
Feedback	+	+						+
Accuracy		+						
Completeness		+						
Fault-tolerance						+		
Resource safety								
Readability							+	+
Controllability						+	+	+
Navigability	+	+				+	+	+
Simplicity							+	+
Privacy						+		+
Security						+		
Insurance						+		
Familiarity						+		
Loading time	+							+

By approaching to each measures for the implementation of UCA (artifacts: method, model, construct, instantiation), Jokela (2001) proposed User-Centered Design Performance Assessment (UCD PA) evaluation processes and applied the factors from the viewpoints of quantity, quality and integration to system (software) evaluations. Thereby the processes to the evaluations of the maturity of the usability of mobile products quantity, quality, and integration were applied to the processes.

Along with the development of IT industry, as case studies for certain industries except for the aspect of usability evaluation methodology development, Vergo et al. (2003) suggested the application of user-centered usability evaluation methods for the evaluations of e-Commerce interface design.

Jameson (2003) defined the goals for the evaluation of the usability of user-adaptive systems as predictability or transparency, controllability, carefulness and the width of experiences, and proposed certain evaluation methods.

He concretized them as per figure 13, presenting the differences in positive and negative effects by placing arrows between items for the correction of evaluation results (solid line: positive, dotted line: negative).

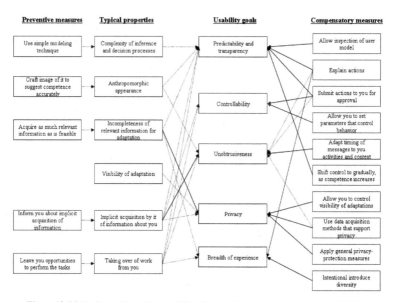

Figure 13. Method to evaluate the usability of user-adaptive systems (Jameson, 2003)

Table 22. Examples of online community evaluation metrics (modified from Preece and Maloney, 2003)

Evaluation concept	Sociability implications (example)	Usability solutions (example)
1. Purpose: Why should I participate in this community?	How should I express necessary information considering what the contents are?	Clear title and purpose should be provided. Graphics should not go out of major messages.
2. Policy: What is the role?	What kind of policy supports the purpose of community?	Should present in clear and simple words, appropriate location.
3. Policy: How should I communicate with other communities?	Newly entering members want to communicate with others in the community but what do existing members want?, How can I satisfy these two groups?	Determines the part of usability support, provides templates, emotions, FAQs, single messages, or digests for listservers, search facilities, ability to send private message (back channel) etc.
4. Purpose: Can I get what I want?	Considering the social requirement of the community, whom is this for?	How to determine the level of communication task.

Also, Preece and Maloney (2003) proposed nine evaluation metrics focused on the evaluation of interactions between sociability and usability for the evaluation of online community, and applied them to practices (table 22).

Although the services and systems formed through inter-personal services and the potential service attitudes and behaviors may be important evaluation factors for ubiquitous services the subjects of this research, usability evaluation guidelines have been contemplated as a part of the method to increase the effect of product uses thus above researches have the weakness of sufficiently considering comprehensive interactivity factors possessed by inter-personal services.

2.2.4 Approaches to inter-personal service quality evaluations

The results of the researches in user behavior areas presented the interactivity occurring from the relations expressed subjective quality, humanistic quality, perceived service quality, functional quality, interaction quality and service delivery as important composing dimensions of service qualities (Barki and Hartwick, 1994). SERVQUAL model (Parasuraman et al., 1988; Parasuraman and Zeithaml, 1994) was proposed as a representative service quality evaluation method for inter-personal services. Through debates with SERVPERF model (Cronin and Taylor, 1992) focused only on service outcomes, revised SERVQUAL model was additionally proposed. However, since SERVQUAL model and its revised model dealt with traditional inter-personal service area, they have limitations in evaluating the system services that are possible in ubiquitous service environments (table 23).

The efforts to evaluate service qualities have been actively made in service science area. If the theory of the research that distinguished between technical qualities and functional qualities, where the methods to evaluate service qualities were presented and the research into SERVPERF (Cronin and Taylor, 1994) that connected perceived service qualities with consumer satisfactions on particular services were representative researches in social science, SERVQUAL proposed by Parasuraman et al. (1988) has been most frequently adopted in the researches from the viewpoint of marketing. Especially, the utilization of the evaluation concepts of SERVQUAL has been expanded to diverse industrial areas by the researches (Parasuraman et al., 1988; Asubonteng et al., 1996; Donnelly and Shiu, 1999).

SERVQUAL has been implemented based on the theory defining the quality of services as 'the gap between the services expected by customers and the services actually perceived by customers', but due to the problems such as the inconsistency in the dimension of evaluations of first evaluation items and the diversity in the interpretation of the concept of expectation, researches doubting its reliability have been continued (Teas, 1994), consequently the researches into the methodologies suitable to particular industrial fields have been attempted (Landrum and Prybutok, 2004).

Especially in information systems area, the attempts to measure the quality of

52

information system services using SERVQUAL have been constantly presented and diverse approaches are being attempted (Watson et al., 1998; Jiang et al., 2002; Landrum and Prybutok, 2004; Kettinger and Lee, 2005; Pitt et al., 2007). SERVQUAL model defined customers' judgment on overall excellence of superiority of products as perceived service quality and defined that service qualities consist of the five dimensions of reliability, responsiveness, empathy, assurance, and tangibility (Nitecki, 1995; Babakus and Boller, 2002; table 24). When it is seen from the proposed viewpoint, ubiquitous services also can evaluate the service quality provided to users thus the attempts to evaluate the quality of ubiquitous services using SERVQUAL model were made (Dyke et al., 1997; Hollemans, 1999).

Table 23. The factors related to user expectation levels in inter-personal services (modified from Carr, 2002)

Factor	Sub-factor	Content
Internal factors	Personal needs	· The factors that can satisfy the needs of self-realization
	Involvement	· When users use services, as involvement increases, the gap between ideal service level and expected service level will be reduced
	Past experience	· Users' past experiences include experiences in particular services, experiences in other services with the same functions and experiences in similar services, and as experiences increase, expectations will be enhanced
External factors	Competitive alternatives	· The level expected from a certain service by a user will be influenced by other functions available to the user
	Social situations	· When users use services together with other users, the level expected by them will be enhanced further
	Words-of-mouth	· Words-of-mouth communication means the behaviors of a users asking about a service to other users or seeking advices from other users before he uses the service
		· The information acquired so plays the role in forming and strengthening the predicted expectation of the customer
Situational factors	Consumer emotion	· Users accept services more easily when their emotions are in good states
	Weather	· Temporary situational factor that plays the role in changing the expectation levels of users
	Temporal restriction	· When there is temporal restriction, users tend to predicted expectations over services

Table 24. Representative dimensions where users evaluate services (modified from Nitecki, 1995; Babakus and Boller, 2002)

Dimension	Definition	Example
Tangibility	External clue to service evaluations.	Users in physical facilities, equipments and service facilities.
Reliability	The ability to accurately implement promised services.	Through service implementations, strict observance of promised time.
Responsiveness	The will to help users and to provide instant services.	Timely services, immediate responses to inquiries or demands, provision of fast services.
Courtesy	Considerations in contact points with users, courteousness.	Consideration about users' time.
Accessibility	Accessibility and easy contacts.	Reduced reservation, waiting time.
Understanding	The efforts to figure out users' needs.	Learning of concrete users' requirements.

Especially, the web site evaluations utilizing SERVQUAL were frequently utilized in online services (Loiacono et al., 2000), and as one of extended models, a research into 'ubi-SERVQUAL' model was executed for the evaluation of ubiquitous services (Kwon and Kim, 2005).

The extended applied model utilized the indices composed of reliability, responsiveness, assurance, and empathy. The proposed research is significant in that it includes not only technical aspects but also behavioral aspects (table 25).

Borriello et al. (2001) extended the concept of inter-personal service evaluations and proposed a research on the evaluation focused on the relationship between human value and ubiquitous services. They presented twelve human values from the aspect of ethics and defined their composing factors as 1) human welfare, 2) ownership and property, 3) freedom from bias, 4) privacy, 5) universal usability, 6) trust, 7) autonomy, 8) informed consent, 9) accountability, 10) identity, 11) calmness, and 12) environmental sustainability.

Table 25. ubi-SERVQUAL: SERVQUAL model for ubiquitous service evaluation (Kwon and Kim, 2005).

Evaluation index	Description
Reliability 1	If ubiquitous technology service providers who are more excellent than information technology service providers promised to provide certain services at given times, they will keep their promises.
Reliability 2	Ubiquitous technology service providers who are more excellent than information technology service providers will provide services successfully from when they begin services.
Reliability 3	Ubiquitous technology service providers who are more excellent than information technology service providers will perform their promises at the times they promised.
Responsiveness 1	Ubiquitous technology service providers who are more excellent than information technology service providers will accurately inform users when the services will be implemented.
Responsiveness 2	The smart software of ubiquitous technology service which is more excellent than the staffs of information technology service providers will provide instant services to users.
Assurance 1	The smart software of ubiquitous technology service which is more excellent than the staffs of information technology service providers will render always the same reliability to users.
Assurance 2	The smart software of ubiquitous technology service which is more excellent than the staffs of information technology service providers will be familiar to users.
Empathy 1	The smart software of ubiquitous technology service which is more excellent than the staffs of information technology service providers will sincerely think of customers' interests.
Empathy 2	The smart software of ubiquitous technology service which is more excellent than the staffs of information technology service providers understands the detailed needs of users.

2.3 Limitations of the literature review

In this research, in order to develop evaluation systems for the interactivity of ubiquitous services, the evaluation methods from the viewpoint of user-centered design, the evaluation methods based on psychometric theory, the methods from the viewpoint of usability evaluations, and the researches related to the background theories and practical applications of the methods from the viewpoint of inter-personal service quality evaluation view point were reviewed (table 26).

Since ubiquitous services not only distribute large numbers of diverse types of devices around users but also aim at the invisible services filtered into environments, the problem of evaluation subjects being increased in number or becoming obscure arises (Newhagen, 1998; Brody and Gottsman, 1999). Thus the evaluations of the usability of particular devices (artifacts) showed limitations.

Table 26. Comparison of the service evaluation method in different perspectives

Approach to evaluation	Evaluation paradigm	Strength	Things to be complemented
Usability evaluation	UCA, UMM (Generic/Process)	· Diverse evaluation methods · Consideration for use environment or user characteristics · Abundant examples of the application of the evaluation	· Obscurity in the range of product or service evaluation · Insufficient inter-personal service evaluation models
Ubiquitous computer evaluation	Ubiquitous system evaluation (Process)	· Performance evaluation in the aspects of HW or SW · Systematic evaluation of large scaled systems	· Insufficient examples of the application of the evaluation · Difficulty in evaluating subjective or inter-personal services
Inter-personal service evaluation	Ubi-SERVQUAL (Generic)	· Diverse verified service quality evaluation methods · Provision of concretized evaluation guidelines	· Limitations in applying to objective or performance evaluations · Wide and obscure range of quality evaluation
Evaluation utilizing psychometrics	Bibliometrics (Generic)	· Systematic method to evaluate user emotions · Provision of diverse components, evaluations and analysis systems	· Difficult to apply the evaluations fast due to complexity in application stages · A lot of preparations are required for application of large scaled systems

Considering the limitation that the measurements of the quality of inter-personal services do not reflect the characteristics of ubiquitous services, the evaluations reflecting the uniqueness of ubiquitous services themselves are executed on the level of concept indicating that they are not suitable to find concrete methods to improve. When evaluation tools were developed based on psychometric theories, the tools were developed by observing user's responses to the experiences in evaluation subjects but the evaluations of interactivity were judged to be not an easy work to do because ubiquitous services are not yet so common for users to experience.

Thorough examinations of users before providing ubiquitous are quite common but following preconditions were extracted in ubiquitous service environments.

- Users do not know accurate concepts of ubiquitous services.
- In order to examine ubiquitous service users, general requirements, not a certain function of human behaviors must be known.
- Commercialized ubiquitous services environments are insufficient, thus large scaled field surveys are difficult.
- The ranges of users who may use ubiquitous services are too wide.
- Even experts have expertise only in the area belonging to their specialized fields in fact, thus the experts in overall ubiquitous services are rare.

The limitations of existing researches related to ubiquitous service evaluation systems contemplated in chapter 2 are as follows.

First, existing evaluation frameworks, the scopes are only applied on the level of the applications of ubiquitous computing (e.g.: middleware, sensor, particular sub-service, systems). The researches on evaluations of overall ubiquitous services, i.e. the researches into the evaluation methods comprising the users constituting ubiquitous services, service systems, input and output devices, were insufficient. And this is interpreted to be the result of the approaches limiting the range of ubiquitous service evaluations by understanding the services as results of use of products assuming ubiquitous services as products along with the limited market of ubiquitous services industries with insufficient generalization. Now, the researches related to user-centered evaluations in ubiquitous services are urgently required even for the development of 'ubiquitous HCI' area.

Second, psychometrics or ubiquitous service characteristic factors for the evaluation of inter-personal services quality not only did not present the process of extraction but also were a 'silo (one direction in cylinder shape)' type approach that just made general service characteristics not reflecting the characteristics of ubiquitous service environments into 'ubiquitous'. It is obvious that if ubiquitous services are evaluated with a silo type approach, there will be limitations by origin in extracting concrete methods of development.

Third, although the usability considering product characteristics of ubiquitous services was required to be extended understanding ubiquitous services as derivative services of inter-personal services, most of the researches were attempts on applying conceptual interactivities to ubiquitous services rather than concrete examples of applications. Especially, the examples of experience, empiricalness, satisfaction and interactions were presented in order to apply extended concepts of usability to practice, also comprehensive approaches comprising these two concepts were insufficient.

Fourth, when ubiquitous computing technologies emerged after the year of 2000, most of existing researches related to ubiquitous services were biased toward only ubiquitous computing technologies. Thus they were focused on the evaluations of key technologies and applications. In most cases, they were finished as researches themselves. Also, after 2005, when ubiquitous technologies began to be commercialized, diverse researches from the business viewpoint are being executed, but only the classifications of ubiquitous services that may be possible according to the criteria of providers are listed. The proposals about the extraction of priorities regarding which service should be actually focused on in providing services to users were insufficient. This is because of the feed-forward, where the implicit needs of ubiquitous service users are actually extracted to be reflected on the services, are not yet applied, and the development of the system of user-centered evaluation methods is urgently required in order to overcome this.

In this study, the understanding of ubiquitous services is to be enhanced by clarifying the concepts of ubiquitous services, and the methods to evaluate user-centered ubiquitous services are to be presented by the evaluation systems related to interactivity through the development of the user-centered evaluation systems for the aspects of inter-personal services and the aspect of usability reflecting the characteristics of ubiquitous service environments.

Part III: Development of ubiquitous service evaluation metric with interactivity

3. Development of interactivity metric to support the designing of user-centered ubiquitous services

3.1 Overview

The importance of 'user-centered' services is being emphasized more in ubiquitous services than in information technology services. The ubiquitous services represented by invisible calm technology and user technology not only support existing methods where services are supported on requests but also support the services where users' intentions and circumstances are grasped and thereby users are actively supported. However, because evaluating the ubiquitous services to be developed later in the state where not all of the key technologies related to ubiquitous have been realized has the limitation of technology oriented realization evaluation, the modeling the method to evaluate ubiquitous service experiences from the viewpoint of users rather than from the viewpoint of developers is required (Chin et al., 1998; Edwards et al., 2003; Fleisch and Tellkamp, 2003).

Like figure 14, the concept of interactivity in ubiquitous services should go out of existing concepts where the interactivity focused on the objective aspect directly connected to the degree of implementation of users and function-based interactivity is emphasized and it should emphasize subjective or emotional aspects and user behavioral aspect, i.e. cognition and activity-based interactivity (Nielsen, 1994; Muirhead, 2001; McMillan and Hwang, 2002).

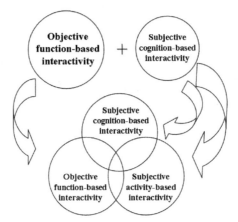

Figure 14. Changes in interactivity in ubiquitous services (modified from Muirhead, 2001; McMillan and Hwang, 2002)

Because the ultimate evaluation of ubiquitous services will be made by users, and the results of user evaluations will be expressed is general satisfaction of the services, sufficient explanations are not possible with only the function-based concept of interactivity in the narrow meaning. Therefore, subjective interactivity was to be expanded to the same level of objective function-based interactivity in order to present the method to evaluate the interactivity of ubiquitous services.

The technologies realizing ubiquitous services do not mean performance itself any more (objective function-based). Table 27 illustrates that the new conceptual ultimate goals of ubiquitous services are in a new dimension rather than enhanced performances, diverse functions and convenience in use.

Table 27. Example of ubiquitous service utilization

Case	Example
Food storage service	Foods are to be stored cool in summer. Our ancestors in the past used stone ice warehouses but now we use refrigerators using electricity and refrigerant. Only the form of stone ice warehouses was changed into refrigerators but the result they attempt to give to humans is not so much different. And refrigerators still maintain the independent form and function as refrigerators. However the refrigerators in u-Service can perceive the kinds, amounts and validities of the foods stored in them and can inform users about what foods are necessary and what foods are to be consumed first. Also, they can even implement the role of receiving medical information of the family to grasp whether the foods necessary for special diet for family members are available and the role of connecting to markets to automatically order foods and pay for the foods. Of course those roles may not be implemented directly by refrigerators, and refrigerators may play a role in the process.

The presented example means that ubiquitous services are not mainly purposed to enhance the performances of independent services any more but are purposed to grasp information related to all devices, services and related information in connection with refrigerators (services), and integrate them in order to provide users with the most appropriate solutions. The solutions here are not the enhancement of hardware performances but the results of users' intellectual and/or behavioral judgments (subjective cognition and/or activity) which mean the results of interactions with services (Cho and Leckenby, 1997; Jo et al., 2006).

Therefore, this research attempted to develop the methods that can appropriately model interactions in ubiquitous service from objective function-based, subjective cognition-based and subjective activity-based perspectives to evaluate them. The development methodology was based on the results of related studies reviewed in Part II and the processes of psychometric theory that are most frequently utilized in the developments of metrics (Parasuraman and Zeithaml, 1994; Lewis, 1995).

3.2 Development procedures

Figure 15 shows the processes of the development of interactivity metric of this study. The approach to this study was composed in two parts. The processes composed of the development of ubiquitous service interactivity attribute index, then the development of interactivity performance measurements were presented in the final metrics where the components of ubiquitous services were considered. The definition of ubiquitous service components referred to the architectures of ubiquitous services. However, the models of appropriate reference examples were insufficient. Thus this study analyzed the components of the services to constitute ubiquitous services such as IT services, inter-personal services, mobile services and system services.

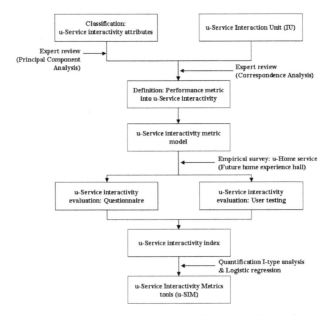

Figure 15. The development procedures of ubiquitous service interactivity metric

The indices collected in literature reviews were integrated to define ubiquitous attribute indices and expert group (policy maker, order placer, designer, developer, standard researcher) reviews were executed to select and structuralize the indices. Interactivity measurement definitions were executed by classifying related indices by analyzing the researches related to usability measurements and ubiquitous service evaluation methods.

The indices extracted and measurements constituted the Evaluation Areas (EA) of ubiquitous service components to finalize the metrics indices. Large scaled user surveys were executed on u-Home services for validation and priority weight estimation. The final metrics were developed as evaluation systems so that they can be readily applied to practices by designers to maximize utility.

3.3 Interactivity attributes in ubiquitous service environments

3.3.1 Composition of attributes

The interactivity attributes in ubiquitous service environments can be defined as the concept of 'how easily can the tasks for ubiquitous service can be executed, and the user be satisfied with results in user environments (Siewiorek, 2002)'. The concept of interactivity attributes can be explained in the objective aspects related to the works executed within the integrated service consisting of ubiquitous service environments, relevant services and users. The results of the researches related to users' subjective aspects were implemented in the areas such as HCI and human factors (ergonomics).

In order to define the interactivity attributes of ubiquitous services, extraction of interactivity attributes through literature reviews, selection and integration of interactivity attributes and hierarchical classification of interactivity attributes were executed.

Table 28. Criteria to extract interactivity attributes of ubiquitous services

Criteria	Content	Examples of application
Selection	Whether it directly exerts influences on interactivity	In the case of learnability, users can easily learn and implement services for sustained use of ubiquitous services. It was selected because it is an index directly influencing service use.
Integration	Whether similar or overlapped concepts exist	In the case of fun, playfulness and addiction, they were integrated because they are the factors of the concepts for users to easily understand the functions or interface methods of ubiquitous services that they learned to enjoy the services.
Deletion	Difficulty in measurement in the aspect of the performances of services or systems	Maintainability is a factor of the requirement that maintenances of services should be easy but this was excluded because this can't be executed in the environment of limited services and because a lot of difficulty is expected in selecting the measurements related to system experts' works with ensured objectivity.

The interactivity attributes of ubiquitous services were classified based on Part II (related studies). A hundred and eighty-six factors related to ubiquitous services and interactivity attributes were extracted.

The attributes of the factors extracted included the attributes with overlapped concepts or the attributes representing subjective emotions or preference rather objective ones. Thus the analyses to extract the attribute indices of objective functional aspects, subjective cognitions and behavioral aspects were executed. A hundred and eighty-six interactivity factors extracted were classified by applying factor selection criteria as shown in table 28.

Also, candidate indices were selected by applying criteria such as the size of attribute concepts, vertical relations and correlations. The size of concepts is explained as the size of the comprehensive or general ranges contained in interactivity factors.

Table 29. First classified factors of ubiquitous service interactivity (31 factors)

No.	Candidate factor	Integrated factor
1	Application robustness	Robustness, Sensitivity, Capability.
2	Compatibility	Social acceptance, Adjustability, Interface quality.
3	Context-awareness	Context of use, Awareness of application capability.
4	Diversity of selection	Source diversity, Selectivity, I/O correspondence.
5	Direction of communication	Synchronicity, Equality of participation, Communication ability, Interaction transparency.
6	Experienceability	Multi-sensory experience, Breadth experience.
7	Fun	Playfulness, Addiction, Likability, Distraction, Attraction.
8	Learnability	Training, Adaptability.
9	Level of effort	Simplicity, Spontaneity, Complexity, User perception.
10	Linking to other systems	Integration, Interoperability, Scalability, Integrability.
11	Location-awareness	Location sensing, Position-awareness, Situation-awareness.
12	Mobility	Nomadicity, Simplicity, Portability, Accessibility.
13	Personalization	Personal information, Personal tailorability, Customizability.
14	Predictability	Predictability of application behavior.
15	Reality	Communication context, Virtual reality.
16	Reliability	Credibility, Accuracy, Trust, Information quality, Confidence in results, Confidence in using the system, Functionality.
17	Responsiveness	Real-time interaction, Intelligent interaction, Transformation, Responsiveness and the perceived purpose of communication, Immediacy of feedback, Feedback or feed-forward, Observability.
18	Safety	Prevention, Privacy.
19	Satisfaction	Interaction quality, Mutuality, Service guarantee.
20	Security	Error traceability, Stability, Maintainability.
21	Suitability	Interoperability, , Sharability, Adoptability.
22	System capability	Performance, Ability, Proactiveness.
23	Time flexibility	Contingency, Degree of contingency, Time sensitivity.
24	Ubiquitous connectivity	Ubiquitous integrity, Real time connectivity, Connectivity.
25	Ubiquity or Pervasiveness	Reversibility, Need for support, Wearability.
26	Understandability	Downloadability, Help or Wizard, On-line help, Helpfulness, Help content, Technical manuals.
27	University	Utility, Ambient intelligibility.
28	Unobtrusiveness	Inferencing, Transparency, Consistency, Compliance, Embeddedness, Dialogue initiative.
29	Usability	Ease of use, Quality of use, Effectiveness, Efficiency, Reusability.
30	User controllability	Controllability, Modifiability.
31	User involvement	Relation immersion, Interaction involvement, User immersion.

For example, in the case of 'efficiency' used to evaluate the efficiency of work executions, it can be considered a priority concept including not only are general the contents but also many concepts such as simplicity of work execution stages, short work execution time, etc. Vertical relations between concepts are defined as the conceptual inclusion of two different interactivity factors in a factor. In example, in the case of 'observability', a requirement that service status must be perceivable to users during service executions.

This can be seen that it is conceptually included in 'responsiveness', a requirement that the responses to interactions between all changes occurring between services and users must be provided. Associations between concepts are explained as causal relations or correlations between the concepts possessed by different interactivity factors. The criteria used when a dialogue initiative and unobtrusivenss are integrated may be given as examples. In case dialogue initiative which is a requirement that artificial restrictions should not be given when users enter certain information into services is embodied in ubiquitous service interfaces, unobtrusiveness which is a requirement that services should maintain appropriateness and should not deviate from certain extents is also ensured, thus these two were integrated. Thirty-one factors were classified based on factor extraction criteria (table 29).

3.3.2 Hierarchical classification of attributes

Thirty-one ubiquitous service interactivity attribute indices first selected and integrated were structuralized through expert survey method. Those were mathematically interpreted through the results of Principal Component Analysis (PCA) and Correspondence Analysis (CA). The surveys were executed by the same evaluators in order to maintain consistency in indices deducing and relation analyses. The expert groups participated were ten subjects (average career: 9.4 years) in total and opinions were converged from diverse areas such as policy makers, order placers, designers, developers and standards researchers (table 30).

Table 30. The expert groups participated in factors structuralizing

Area	Number	Career	Remark
Policy maker	3	10-12 years	Korea Land Corporation (KOLAND), Housing & Urban Research Institute (HURI), Korea Research Institute for Human Settlements (KRIHS)
Project planner	2	8/13 years	Special Purpose Companies (SPC), Project Financing (PF) group
Designer/Architect	2	7/9 years	IT service company
Developer	2	5/8 years	Telecom/communication company
Standards researcher	1	11 years	Telecommunications Technology Association (TTA)

In the expert group surveys, the cases where there were relations between attributes were recorded as '2', the cases where relations between principles were obscure were recorded as '1', and the cases where there was no relation between principles were recorded as '0'. The questionnaires for the expert surveys were prepared using upper orthogonal matrix input format (Kim, 2003).

Table 31. The attribute indices deduced with major component analysis

Representative attribute	Description
Contextualization support	· Related to ubiquitous service environments · The level of the interactions considering the relations between services and users · The level of the provision of customized services through status perceptions
Service capability support	· Related to the ability to provide ubiquitous services · The level of ubiquitous service user protection and error prevention · The level of the performance, speed, security and storage ability of service systems
Ubiquity support	· The extent of the ubiquity of ubiquitous services · Ubiquitous connectivity of services and convenience in carrying devices etc.
User experience support	· The extent of user experiences in the use of ubiquitous services · User participation and the degree of effort for use of ubiquitous services · The communication direction or response level of ubiquitous service users

Major component analyses were done by repeating varimax with Kaiser normalization rotation sixteen times utilizing SAS 6.0, and since this method investigates the extent of explanation based on the values with 1 or greater eigenvalues to establish indices, the variables that can have 80% or larger explanation ability were defined among the values with 1 or greater eigenvalue based on the content of the results (for the detailed results on PCA, see Appendix C). Because, the analyses considering all variables become more difficult as the number of variables increases (Lattin et al., 2003), the representative values that can represent the variables in less number of variables were extracted. Four attribute indices with the explanation ability of 79.3% were extracted by analyzing major components (table 31).

Thirty-one attribute indices included in the final list of interactivity factors were represented by four representative indices, and the attributes of the indices were classified as function-based or cognition-based interactivities (figure 16).

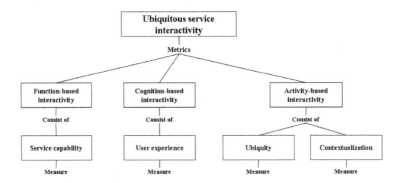

Figure 16. Ubiquitous service interactivity evaluation structure

Table 32. Classification of ubiquitous service interactivity

Interactivity	Definition
Function-based	Focused on various functions possessed by the services enabling users' interactions.
Cognition-based	Focused on the subjective judgment on how much users feel the interactivity of services.
Activity-based	Focused on the will or tendency to interact based on users' experiences.

The definitions of function, cognition, and activity-based interactivities of finally classified systems are as per table 32.

Also, the definitions of the indices from ubiquitous service interactivity evaluation areas are as per table 33. Especially, contextualization means the changes of the services of certain use environments (context of use) in their characteristics which are a very important characteristic in complex ubiquitous service environments where services must be provided by automatically perceiving changes in users' attitudes (profiles).

3.4 Development of metric for ubiquitous service interactivity

Once the interactivity attributes of ubiquitous services have been defined, the measurement values that can evaluate the interactivity of ubiquitous services are required. Interactivity metric (performance measure) means the measures to determine the levels of interactivity factors comprising the indices indicating what measurement values should be used to evaluate the extents of interactivity. Large scaled researches into measurement values were executed in the areas of human factors (ergonomics), psychology and behavioral science, and most of which were related to the works of users to use products. On the other hand, the researches in the measurement values of interactivity were mainly executed as the researches quantifying users' subjective views (Zack, 1993; Won and Lee, 2007).

Table 33. Evaluation areas by interactivity attributes

EA (Evaluation Area) 1st level	EA (Evaluation Area) 2nd level	Definition/Description
Service capability	Agility	· Means the speed and capability of works when wanted functions are executed in using the services
	Time flexibility	· Means the ability related to the time after receiving a users input until the services show a response
	Error prevention	· Means whether there are the methods to prevent mistakes or errors occurring in using services
User experience	Fun	· Means the extent to which a user considers the activity of using certain services as compensation when he uses services
	Level of effort	· The contents of services provided are differentiated based on the level of users' efforts and in the case of basic services this means the extent to which users' efforts can be minimized
	Experienceability	· Means interests or preferences of individuals and whether appropriate information is provided based on past experiences
Contextualization	Responsiveness	· Means the extent to which service requests are responded fast and accurately
	Unobtrusiveness	· Means how easily and conveniently the devices to be provided with services can be dealt and used
	User involvement	· Means how accurately and autonomously services can be provided without being helped by users enabling users to be involved
Ubiquity	Connectivity	· Means how many services can be accessed simultaneously
	Real time communication	· Means how many services can be accessed in a short period of time
	User controllability	· Means the extent to which other sub-services provided prior to a provision of a service to provide the service when a users uses a service are reliable

The most important in extracting the measurement values of interactivity is whether the measurement values are suitable to evaluate the levels of relevant factors because if uncorrelated measurement values are selected, the evaluations of interactivity factors become insignificant. This research was executed in the fashion of existing studies where measurement values were analyzed to extract all the lists selectable as measurement values, and subsequently determine their correlations with factors.

3.4.1 Classification of interactivity factor measurement values

Interactivity measurement values mean the results obtained through measurements in order to quantitatively express the interactivity factors related to ubiquitous services or indirect evaluation results. In example, the number of interfaces or functions, the number of task stages, the time consumed varying with changes in environments, accuracy of perceptions used when works are executed by users for actual services in order to evaluate the extent of contextualization which is one of interactivity factors can be said to be the interactivity factor measurement values related to contextualization.

In order to define the measurement values to quantify the extent of the interactivity of ubiquitous services, eighty initial indices were collected. But the initial indices that were insufficient to evaluate ubiquitous services such as the ones involving the factors closer to the measurement values of emotional factor, i.e. preference or the ones with obscure abstract levels or measurements of software performances were excluded. In order to extract the measurement values related to interactivity factors, the measurement values with close relations to interactivity factors were first selected, and the measurement values which were higher concepts than the measurement values of similar concepts were unified into one. Also the measurement values with obscure measurement methods and the measurement values related to bio-signal were excluded.

3.4.2 Definition of ubiquitous service components

The researches related to the evaluation ranges for the measurement of ubiquitous service interactivity have been executed centered on designers and evaluators but the user-centered guidelines related to ubiquitous service system evaluation defined by Telecommunication Technology Association (TTA) carry a great significance in that they selected more user-centered diverse measurement ranges of applications themselves and software (Davies and Gellersen, 2002).

For the development of user-centered ubiquitous interactivity evaluation system which is the goal of this study, interaction units (Ryu et al., 2006) were defines as four components and eight attribute constituents (table 34). The behaviors of users perceiving and manipulating service functions are recognized by input devices to call relevant services. Service systems integrate the requested functions to interpret them and capsulate them to be prepared for provisions. Once the preparation to provide the services suitable to use environments is completed, the services personalized for individual users are browsed and provided.

As a method to easily express the behaviors of the dynamic architectures of service systems, the 'control theory' (Hassanein and Head, 2003; Franze et al., 2006; Ryu et al., 2006), widely defined in the area of engineering and mathematics, was referred to in order to package research frameworks into control loop as per figure 17.

Table 34. The range of ubiquitous service interactivity evaluation unit

Interaction Unit (IU)		Definition
User	·Perception ·Manipulation	·The measurement value evaluated by the subjective judgments of users ·This means users' subjective judgments and/or perceptions at the time of the first use of services but once the interactions with services began ·This means the measurement values including users' experiences
Input artifacts	·Recognition ·Service call	·The tasks that directly require services, are directly associated with users' works and can be objectively measured are included
Service systems	·Integration ·Capsulation	·The measurement value of changes in systems measured in order to provide services for the requirements and/or needs of users
Output artifacts	·Browsing & Execution ·Personalization	·This means the environments and/or outcomes where user are provided with services including the results of concrete tasks provided to users as the results of service systems

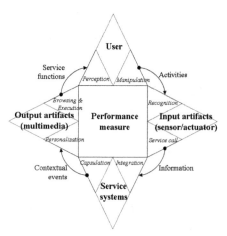

Figure 17. Control loop framework for the evaluation of u-Service interactivity

3.4.3 Classification of measurement values by u-Service components

In order to realize concrete methods for ubiquitous service interactivity evaluation, the selection of the design variables that can be evaluated and the methods to evaluate them are necessary. In this study, the structure of the metrics for the diagnoses of the level of ubiquitous interactivity was proposed. The indices deduced from preliminary studies and empirical studies were two-hundred and fifty-six (for the detailed indexes on the survey datasets, see Appendix D) in total. An In-Depth Interview (IDI) method was executed for the selection of the indices considering the characteristics of ubiquitous services and for mapping by evaluation area components. The evaluation indices considering the evaluation criteria required for the evaluation of ubiquitous interactivity and design related variables were selected. In order to evaluate ubiquitous service interactivity and associations between service evaluation factors, the service evaluation indices judged to be able to be evaluated consistently with each of interactivities by many experts were determined. Associations indicate how important service evaluation factors are in determining the levels of interactivity. Among existing researches into various methodologies, collaborations between users and design experts and IDI method were shown to be useful and reliable measures (Bruseberg and Philip, 2001).

The IDI was executed on eight persons (five males, three females) in human factors (ergonomics) or cognitive science through one-to-one marking method. The subjects had master degrees or higher education's, had practical experiences in any of the areas of human factors (ergonomics) or cognitive science, and were selected because they were judged as having the concept related to ubiquitous services and implementing related works. Interviews took place at Human Interface Systems (HIS) laboratory of Seoul National University and workplace of each person. The interview lasted seven days from May 4th to 11th, 2007, and the interviews were done twice for each person (table 35). As for the type of questions of IDI, a grand tour type question was avoided and semi-structured format question was selected where opinions could be submitted freely for necessary sections but must be written in (Guion, 2006).

Table 35. General characteristics of the participants in In-Depth Interview (IDI)

Case	Gender	Career	Remark
1	Male	Doctor in human factors (ergonomics), 15 years in related area, working in a university.	
2	Male	Doctor in human factors (ergonomics), 8 years in related area, working in an IT manufacturing laboratory.	
3	Male	Doctor in human factors (ergonomics), 5 years in related area, working in a university laboratory.	
4	Male	Master in human factors (ergonomics), 5 years in related area, working in a government under a public organization.	Policy planner
5	Female	Master in human factors (ergonomics), 5 years in related area, working in an IT standardization laboratory.	
6	Male	Master in human factors (ergonomics), 3 years in related area, working in a laboratory under a public organization.	Policy planner
7	Female	Master in human factors (ergonomics), 3 years in related area, working in an IT manufacturing business.	Service architect
8	Female	Master in cognitive science, 3 years in related area, working in a IT manufacturing business.	Service provider

First, IDI selected the indices suitable to service attributes. Eighty candidate variables were selected to elect fifty-one metrics for ubiquitous interactivity evaluations. Table 36 shows a metric table consisting of measurement areas (component), characteristics (attribute), evaluation measures for characteristics (indicator), methods of evaluations (metric), and descriptions of evaluation methods (derived measure). These were defined as comprehensive evaluation indices comprising objective and subjective evaluation indices. Fifty-one metrics consisted of ten to fourteen for each component and consisted of design variables (engineering variables) and subjective evaluation indices that could complement each other.

Second, IDI executed the process of mapping selected indices by ubiquitous service attributes. Corresponding fifty-one metrics to four ubiquitous service attribute evaluation indices was executed by preparing the ubiquitous service attribute relevant to each candidate variables in the order of one to ten. From the indices determined by the results, interactivity indices were selected, and the most frequently selected indices to select evaluation indices for each attribute. The deduced ubiquitous service interactivity attribute indices and defined interactivity measurement value indices were integrated to define the final metrics. Table 36 and table 37 present the metrics matrix for ubiquitous service interactivity evaluation.

Table 36. Interactivity of ubiquitous service metric (bold and italic: variable name)

Measurable criteria			Metric	Derived measure	Source (modified/adopted)
Component	Attribute	Indicator			
u-Service user	User expectation level in relation with u-Service functions (Perception)	Agreement degree of service functions (SC: Service Concordance): ratio of expected service functions and the results. *(u₁)*	SC (Service Concordance) = A/B	· A=Number of expected and comprehended service functions · B=Number of functions provided from ubiquitous service	Constantine and Lockwood (1999)
		Participation degree of bi-directional communication, while using service. *(u₂)*	Degree (questionnaire & user testing)	· User's participating degree for bi-directional communication of ubiquitous service	-
		Immersion degree in the service without own location-awareness, while using service. *(u₃)*	Degree (questionnaire & user testing)	· User's immersion degree in ubiquitous service	Scholtz (2006)
		The degree of understanding input data and expecting output at service request. *(u₄)*	A/B or degree (questionnaire & user testing)	· A=Number of expectable and performable I/O · B=Number of I/O provided from ubiquitous service	ISO 25000 (2005)
		The degree of receiving unexpected service by providing unrequested service functions. *(u₅)*	Degree (questionnaire & user testing)	· Whether the implicit needs of ubiquitous service user is to be provided or not	-
		Recognized degree of wasting time while service use. *(u₆)*	Degree (questionnaire & user testing)	· Recognized degree of wasting time during using ubiquitous service	-
	User's efforts required within u-Service use (Perception)	User's approved time before using the service. *(u₇)*	Mean time	· User's approved time before using the service	ISO 9126-4 (2001)
		Learning time to use new service functions. *(u₈)*	Mean time	· Learning time to use new service functions	ISO 9126-3 (2001)
		Time of user spending in hesitation or holding to use the service. *(u₉)*	Mean time or mean number	· Time and frequency of hesitating or holding in using the service	Bertoa et al. (2006)
		Number of user out-of-controls during service use. *(u₁₀)*	Mean number	· Number of being uncontrollable system during operating service	-
		Ratio to change the service contents properly to user's preference or habit automatically. *(u₁₁)*	A/B	· A=Number of service functions changed automatically · B=Number of I/O provided from ubiquitous service environment	Ryu et al. (2006)
		Required time or degree for user to modify the service function procedure in user's convenience. *(u₁₂)*	Mean time or degree (questionnaire & user testing)	· Degree of modifiable service procedure in user's convenience	-
	Cognizance degree of economical response to u-Service (Perception)	Distance degree that user must move additionally to receive the service at proper place and time. *(u₁₃)*	Service moving distance = Dm Degree (questionnaire & user testing)	· Dm=User's moving distance for execution of specific service function · Proper degree of user for the movement distance	- -
		Range degree of physical spaces to recognize the status of the service. *(u₁₄)*	Degree (questionnaire & user testing)	· Proper degree of recognizable range to the status of provided ubiquitous service	Friedewald et al. (2005)
		Ratio of error occurrence during service use. *(u₁₅)*	A/B	· A=Number of service error · B=Number of executing service	UbiComp02 (2002)

	Cognizance degree of efficient response to u-Service (Perception)	Degree of accomplish the purpose of using the service. (u_{16})	Degree (questionnaire & user testing)	· Matching degree of ubiquitous service to the purpose of the user	ISO 15939 (2002)
		Pride or sympathy degree for the service result. (u_{17})	Degree (questionnaire & user testing)	· Pride degree of quality for the result of the requested service or sympathy degree of the result	-
		Frequency of success at requesting the service. (u_{18})	A/B	· A=Number of successful operations of ubiquitous service functions · B=Number of access attempts to ubiquitous service	Bertoa et al. (2006)
	Interface element characteristic of u-Service input device (Manipulation)	Number or consistency degree of interfaces leading user's mistake. (u_{19})	1-(A/B)	· A=Number of functions or message in discord with user's expectation · B=Number of service functions or messages	-
		Design suitability of input devices (look & feel degree). (u_{20})	Degree (questionnaire & user testing)	· Favorable and preferable degree of service input device design (look & feel, touch feel, color, etc.)	-
		Suitability of weight and size of input devices. (u_{21})	Degree (questionnaire & user testing)	· Grip interface to use service input device (weight, size, etc.)	-
		Application degree of visual or voice interface. (u_{22})	Degree (questionnaire & user testing)	· Application degree of multimodal interface	-
		Other services usable degree with one device (one device, multi use). (u_{23})	Mean number	· Number of usable service functions with single device	Ryu et al. (2006)
		Possibility degree of executing multitasking operation. (u_{24})	Degree (questionnaire & user testing)	· Application degree of input device for multitask performance	-
		Portability degree of input device to use the service. (u_{25})	Degree (questionnaire & user testing)	· Portability degree considering use time (relating to battery), size, weight, etc. of portable artifacts	-
u-Service input artifacts (sensor, actuator)	Various (multimodal) input artifacts characteristic to use u-Service (Recognition)	Usable input method or various interactivity degrees (keyboard, stylus, audio input, touch screen, etc.). (i_1)	Mean number or degree (questionnaire & user testing)	· Type, applicable degree of multimodal interface	-
		Usable degree of multimodal devices same service functions. (i_2)	Degree (questionnaire & user testing)	· Applicable degree of same function with multimodal interface	-
		Usable range of requesting the service (sensing distance). (i_3)	Service coverage distance = Dc	· Dc=Successful distance based on user's location	Seffah et al. (2006)
			Degree (questionnaire & user testing)	· Recognizable degree of use for the usable distance	-
		At request of specific service function, modifiable degree with various devices (e.g.: touch screen-remote control). (i_4)	A/B or degree (questionnaire & user testing)	· A=Number of reduced steps to execute the function after modifying the service function · B=Number of steps to execute the function before modifying the service function	ISO 9126-3 (2001)

	Service function level to require u-Service (Service call)	Spending time to execute the input of the next service function. *(i₅)*	Tc-Ts	· Tc= Completion time of executed specific service function · Ts= Start time of specific service function to perform	UbiComp01 (2001)
			Degree (questionnaire & user testing)	· Effort degree of waiting to execute specific service function	-
		Number of requiring modification to execute service due to difference of technology, at using two devices and more. *(i₆)*	Mean number	· Number of changing device to complete the service function execution due to technology	Seffah et al. (2006)
		Number of other input devices that must be referred to complete the execution of service function. *(i₇)*	Mean number	· Number of input devices required for phased execution to complete the interaction with ubiquitous service (the completion of ubiquitous service execution)	Rubin (1994)
		Phase ratio required for requested service function. *(i₈)*	N/Tt	· N=Executing phase to execute specific function of ubiquitous service · Tt=Number of total service task	-
		Suitable degree of system response upon service request (tedium, admittable time degree). *(i₉)*	Degree (questionnaire & user testing)	· Suitable degree of system response during service requests (maximum admittable time of use to endure)	-
		Time rates to find the specific command function. *(i₁₀)*	A/UOT	· A=Time to find specific function during executing service function · UOT=User Operating Time	Basu et al. (2001)
u-Service systems	Unitability or adjustability among u-Service components (Integration)	Suitability ratio of service functions: number of problem occurrence or number of total functions. *(s₁)*	Number of conflicts = A/B	· A=Number of ubiquitous service functions occurred error · B=Total number of ubiquitous service functions	Scholtz and Consolvo (2004)
		Data adjustable degree between service in operating and the component of other services. *(s₂)*	Degree (questionnaire & user testing)	· Data adjustable degree with detail service relating to specific service (e.g.: accuracy of items in refrigerator and recipe to cook)	-
		Acknowledgment degree of service defense system against trespassing of other user. *(s₃)*	Mean number or degree (questionnaire & user testing)	· Suitability of service defense system for other user's access (e.g.: stop of function, warning, etc.)	Lin et al. (1997)
	Capability of providing information of u-Service system (Capsulation)	Stability degree of service system when adding or removing a service function. *(s₄)*	1-(A/B)	· A=Response time of ubiquitous service after adding new HW or SW · B=Response time of ubiquitous service before adding new HW or SW	-
		Suitability of temporary storage saving to provide requested function (buffering degree). *(s₅)*	Degree (questionnaire & user testing)	· Performance degree of temporary storage saving data before being browsed	UbiComp02 (2002)
		Suitability of providing guide usable by multi-user. *(s₆)*	Degree (questionnaire & user testing)	· Suitability of guide available for users with various characteristics	Scholtz (2006)

u-Service output artifacts (multimedia)	Accuracy level of the u-Service result (Browsing & Execution)	Instinctive understandability degree of the service function result. (o_1)	Degree (questionnaire & user testing)	· Availability or degree of instinctive understanding for provided ubiquitous service	Constantine and Lockwood (1999)
		Frequency or number of service system error during using service. (o_2)	Mean number	· Frequency or number of user's error during using the service	Burrell et al. (2002)
		Number of requesting help to confirm the specific output device result. (o_3)	Mean number	· Number of requesting help to confirm the specific service result	Arnstein et al. (2006)
		Suitability degree of service feedback felt by user. (o_4)	Degree (questionnaire & user testing)	· Suitability of service result including the suitability of waiting time, etc.	-
		Required time until completion of loading specific service function. (o_5)	Response time = (A-B)	· A=Providing time of service result · B=Completion time of service command	-
		Stopping or canceling time ratio at providing service. (o_6)	A/UOT	· A=Stop or cancel time at ubiquitous service · UOT=User Operating Time	Seffah et al. (2006)
	Personaliza-bility degree of u-Service user (Personaliza-tion)	Providability degree of differential service for each multi-user. (o_7)	Degree (questionnaire & user testing)	· Multiplicity degree of service result considering the user's characteristics, if there are many users	-
		Modifying degree of help function in accordance with the change of user's environment. (o_8)	Degree (questionnaire & user testing)	· Changing degree of usage result according to the changes of use environment of same user (e.g.: living room via kitchen)	-
		Number of times available to modify the system according to user's preference. (o_9)	Personalization number (mean number)	· Number of modifiable functions by user's preference	Scholtz et al. (2002)
		Suitability of service reaction relating to an unsuitable command (outsider, etc.). (o_{10})	Access controllability = A/B	· A=Number of traceability by executing unsuitable method · B=Number of performing unsuitable method to execute specific service	ISO 9126-2 (2001)
			Degree (questionnaire & user testing)	· Degree of service reaction relating to an unsuitable command	-

Table 37. Evaluation factors of ubiquitous service interactivity
(S: Subjective measure, O: Objective measure)

Measurable criteria		The characteristics indicator of u-service interactivity (characteristic factor)	y_1 (user experience) Participation or effort level of user to use the service	y_2 (contextualization) Provides services adequate to the situation, considered the relation of service and user	y_3 (ubiquity) Portability and pervasive connectedness	y_4 (service capability) Level of user protection and error prevention
u-Service user	User expectation level in relation with u-Service functions (Perception)	Agreement degree of service functions (SC: Service Concordance): ratio of expected service functions and the results. (u_1)	O	-	-	-
		Participation degree of bi-directional communication, while using service. (u_2)	S	-	-	-
		Immersion degree in the service without own location-awareness, while using service. (u_3)	S	-	-	-
		The degree of understanding input data and expecting output at service request. (u_4)	S/O	-	-	-
		The degree of receiving unexpected service by providing unrequested service functions. (u_5)	-	S	-	-
		Recognized degree of wasting time while service use. (u_6)	-	S	-	-
	User's efforts required within u-Service use (Perception)	User's approved time before using the service. (u_7)	O	-	-	-
		Learning time to use new service functions. (u_8)	O	-	-	-
		Time of user spending in hesitation or hold to use the service. (u_9)	O	-	-	-
		Number of user out-of-controls during service use. (u_{10})	O	-	-	-
		Ratio to change the service contents properly to user's preference or habit automatically. (u_{11})	-	O	-	-
		Required time or degree for user to modify the service function procedure in user's convenience. (u_{12})	-	S/O	-	-
	Cognizance degree of economical response to u-Service (Perception)	Distance degree that user must move additionally to receive the service at proper place and time. (u_{13})	-	S/O	-	-
		Range degree of physical spaces to recognize the status of the service. (u_{14})	-	S	-	-
		Ratio of error occurrence during service use. (u_{15})	-	O	-	-

	Cognizance degree of efficient response to u-Service (Perception)	Degree of accomplish the purpose of using the service. (u_{16})	-	S	-	-
		Pride or sympathy degree for the service result. (u_{17})	-	S	-	-
		Frequency of success at requesting service. (u_{18})	-	O	-	-
	Interface element characteristic of u-Service input device (Manipulation)	Number or consistency degree of interfaces leading mistake. (u_{19})	-	-	O	-
		Design suitability of input devices (look & feel degree). (u_{20})	-	-	S	-
		Suitability of weight and size of input devices. (u_{21})	-	-	S	-
		Application degree of visual/voice I/F. (u_{22})	-	-	S	-
		Other services usable degree with one device (one device, multi use). (u_{23})	-	-	O	-
		Possibility degree of executing multitasking operation. (u_{24})	-	-	S	-
		Portability degree of input device to use the service. (u_{25})	-	-	S	-
u-Service input artifacts	Various (multimodal) input artifacts characteristic to use u-Service (Recognition)	Usable input method or various interactivity degrees (keyboard, audio input, touch screen, etc.). (i_1)	-	-	S/O	-
		Usable degree of multimodal devices same service functions. (i_2)	-	-	S	-
		Usable range of requesting the service (sensing distance). (i_3)	-	-	S/O	-
		At request of specific service function, modifiable degree with various devices (e.g.: touch screen-remote control). (i_4)	-	-	S/O	-
	Service function level to require u-Service (Service call)	Spending time to execute the input of the next service function. (i_5)	S/O	-	-	-
		Number of requiring modification to execute service due to difference of technology, at using two devices and more. (i_6)	O	-	-	-
		Number of other input devices that must be referred to complete the execution of service function. (i_7)	O	-	-	-
		Phase ratio required for requested service function. (i_8)	O	-	-	-
		Suitable degree of system response upon service request (tedium, admittable time). (i_9)	S	-	-	-
		Time rates to find the specific command function. (i_{10})	O	-	-	-

Category	Characteristic	Metric				
u-Service systems	Unitability or adjustability among u-Service components (Integration)	Suitability ratio of service functions: number of problem occurrence or number of total functions. *(s₁)*	-	-	-	O
		Data adjustable degree between service in operating and the component of other services. *(s₂)*	-	-	-	S
		Acknowledgment degree of service defense system against trespassing of other user. *(s₃)*	-	-	-	S/O
	Capability of providing information of u-Service system (Capsulation)	Stability degree of service system when adding or removing a service function. *(s₄)*	-	-	-	O
		Suitability of temporary storage saving to provide requested function (buffering degree). *(s₅)*	-	-	-	S
		Suitability of providing guide usable by multi-user. *(s₆)*	-	-	-	S
u-Service output artifacts	Accuracy level of the u-Service result (Browsing & Execution)	Instinctive understandability degree of the service function result. *(o₁)*	-	S	-	-
		Frequency or number of service system error during using service. *(o₂)*	-	-	-	O
		Number of requesting help to confirm the specific output device result. *(o₃)*	-	-	-	O
		Suitability degree of service feedback felt by user. *(o₄)*	-	S	-	-
		Required time until completion of loading specific service function. *(o₅)*	-	-	-	O
		Stopping or canceling time ratio at providing service. *(o₆)*	-	-	-	O
	Personalizability degree of u-Service user (Personalization)	Providability degree of differential service for each multi-user. *(o₇)*	-	-	-	S
		Modifying degree of help function in accordance with the change of user's environment. *(o₈)*	-	-	-	S
		Number of times available to modify the system according to user's preference. *(o₉)*	-	-	-	O
		Suitability of service reaction relating to an unsuitable command (outsider, etc.). *(o₁₀)*	-	-	-	S/O

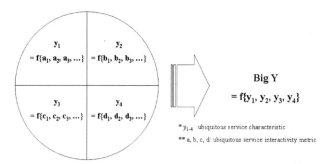

Figure 18. The conceptual model for ubiquitous service interactivity

It is understood to have the structure as figure 18 with influence variable, as a candidate variable, related to ubiquitous service interactivity by applying selected metrics.

In the model of ubiquitous service interactivity, measured variables become independent variables, and the characteristically factor of ubiquitous service become dependent variable, and it defines interactivity as the final dependent variable. In the following case study, it will examine the meaning of proposed variables, eliminate the meaningless variables, and propose influence variables. In addition, it will analyze influence of each influential variable for ubiquitous service interactivity and propose the model.

4. Case study: Interactivity evaluation of u-Home service

4.1 Overview

The case study is performed with two purposes. The first is to examine the relation for each factor of proposed metrics and investigate the priority among factors. In other words, it is to investigate the relation between the attributes of ubiquitous service interactivity and measured values, and to deduce the priority of assessing factors to provide the weights of the priority determination at service designing the planning. The second purpose is to develop conceptual modeling for ubiquitous service interactivity. It would establish the system that allows the easy formulation of user assessment by modeling interactivity of ubiquitous service in the perspective of the user rather than the developers.

Interactivity attribute factors of deduced ubiquitous service have a strong advantage that they are of a synthetic and systematic (mutually exhaustive and comprehensive) type of classification including all sorts of abstractable factors. When evaluating the interactivity for the target service, however, it is not appropriate for circulative design progress to consider all components with equivalent priority (Westwater and Johnson, 1995). That is, when the assessment is to be performed with less labor and cost, the evaluator has a desire to select more important and weighted factors. That is the reason of requiring the information such as priority and priority level of the proposed metrics.

The u-Home service has been selected as a target service applying the metrics case study of ubiquitous service interactivity. The first reason of selection is the u-Home service deems to approach the most practical use level, beyond the conceptual level of ubiquitous service. Actually, there are a number of cases on application to commercial products in 2006, and the new service continues to be studied (Ham, 2006). As of the second reason, it is relatively easy to obtain a concrete experimental space of providing direct experience of ubiquitous service. Since the ubiquitous service constitutes not in small-size laboratories but in big-size buildings or mobile spaces, there are physical and economical limitations on installing a test-bed integrated real-like. The u-Home service, however, has a merit of availability of service selection to give an experience in person to the user with numerous virtual experience centers (government and/or civilian).

4.2 Introduction of u-Home service

Home is the world only for user constituted with people, spaces, environments, furniture, equipments, artifacts, ornaments, etc. (Intille, 2002). All constituted elements provide the optimal context to share the general characteristics responding users' requirements and preferences and to assist the action. The ubiquitous home service (hereinafter, u-Home), mixed with the concept of home and intelligence, is the realized ubiquitous environment at home. Namely, it means the unitive environment, which controls home from the remote place or outside of home by integrating with digital multi-media technology and provides home service relating to user technology or user engineering (Vredenburg, 2002). Since the origin of all environments that human has comes from home, u-Home can be a representative case of developing user-centered design service. The u-Home service has proceeded to change as internet disseminated what into user's life and to introduce information apartments integrated with information, communication, or broadcast (integration). With these, a space providing services by merging people, objects and computer together (convergence) is built (Dey, 2001). The word used variously as intelligent home, smart home or digital home, tends to be representative of u-Home (home-centered design) (table 38). It provides not only 'home' as physical meaning, but also various services what user needs for safety, comfortableness, and convenience, and satisfies human desires (Kakihara and Sorensen, 2002).

In u-Home service environment, home information appliances are connected to a wired or wireless home network. The supported family services shared with individual users: through an own server in the house, can receive services of controlling and managing energy as well as security, guard, shopping, education, or medical services.

Table 38. u-Home service paradigm

New integration technology	Home automation systems (~2000)	Home network systems (2001~)	Ubiquitous home service (2004~)
Wired internet	*Home automation* · Door or window	-	-
Convergence or divergence	-	*Remote control* · Wired phone · Gas valve · Lighting control	*Contents* · Entertainment · Education
Wireless internet	-	*System linkage* · CCTV · Parking lot control · Remote inspection	*Ubiquitous* · Contents services · BcN or wireless internet

Friedewald et al. (2005) have defined the roles of restraint or adjustment (control), entertainment and information as components to embody a service of intelligent environment for home use (AmI: Ambient Intelligent), and proposed service systems providing the service. The differences between providing intelligent home (u-Home) service and home network service (IT service) are indicated in three different kinds, and it is insisted that the development of service providing convenience and usability for user in living or residing spaces is required (table 39).

Table 39. Comparing between IT-service and u-Service in home service systems (modified from Ross and Burnett, 2001; Freidewald et al., 2005)

IT service	Ubiquitous service
· PC based interface, read, write	· Context interface, intuitive, sense
· 'Text' based information	· 'Context' based knowledge
· The construction of home network systems in the center of devices, such as wall-pad, home gateway, etc.	· Implementation of u-Home service based on the interlocking with ubiquitous district service
· Build home network system in the center of information home appliance control and security systems	· Provide elegant, differential service (one-card service, hotel service) through ubiquitous computing infrastructure
· Lack of interlocking service henceforth by individual infra induction for each district	· Convenient service use linked with u-City integrated operation infrastructure

As the time spent at home increases more than any other spaces and the applicable field of u-Home service becomes very wide, the study for the major function required to provide the service is in progress. Edwards and Grinter (2001) have proposed a world model designed to allow the function exchanging information among objects (Machine To Machine: M2M), user recognition (sensing), and auto acquirement of using environment (context). Alahuhta and Heinonen (2003) have presented service environment elements with four types (table 40). The main idea of Home Automation (HA) is to provide easier automation by integration of controls for functions (e.g.: heating, plumbing, ventilation, air-conditioning, lighting, electrical and other installations (fire and burglar alarms, control of electronic appliances)). In intelligent home, it is controlled by touch panels, voice, and hand gestures, face expression, etc.

The conceptual diagram of u-Home accentuating the role of control, entertainment and information is as figure 19. A u-Home service has been advanced with a focus on how the user's required function can be provided, and the case study is performed targeting various u-Home services implemented on these conceptual prolongations.

Table 40. Basic functions and constitution factors of u-Home service (modified from Alahuhta and Heinonen, 2003)

Basic function	Component
Home automation	·Basic housing supportive functions, Security, Support of the independent living
Communication and socialization	·Person to person, Person to community, New forms of socialization
Rest, refreshing, entertainment and sport	·Rest and relaxation, Refreshing and hygiene, Entertainment and hobbies, Sport and fitness
Working and learning	·Household work, Maintenance work, Home office work

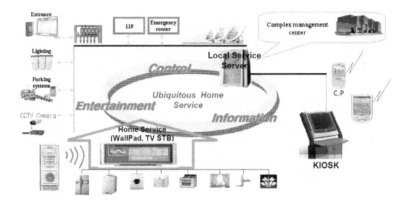

Figure 19. u-Home service configuration (modified from Edwards et al., 2003)

4.3 Experiment design

4.3.1 Questionnaires development

With metric developed in chapter 3, to define user's psychological anchor, questionnaires required for experiment have been created. To assign at least over two questions for each evaluation factor, a total of fifty-four questions are developed. The experiment is executed by completing these in the form of questionnaire. The questionnaire has been provided with two types of task-driven assessment and element-driven assessment. The task-driven assessment has been based on task-scenario, and the element-driven assessment has focused on objective performance of ubiquitous service constitution elements.

The questions of interactivity are about bi-directional communication between service and user occurring when user controls specific service or product. Especially in ubiquitous service environment, to assess the interactivity of services or products, it has developed a method of heuristic evaluation, i.e. one of usable evaluation methods. Since these factors or guides, however, are considered as a part of ways to improve the effects of service or product, inclusive interactivity factors of general service could not be fully considered. For example, the reliability of the service may be increased by successful service use, and psychological anchor for user to understand other services based on the result can be created, but these complexities have not been included in interactivity guideline. Therefore, the questionnaire including psychological anchor has been created with the proposed metric in study.

4.3.2 Selection of experimental targets and definition of user tasks

The experimental target of the study is u-Home service, which provides concrete result of ubiquitous service and has a value more than just a house. The 'future housing gallery', the experimental target, has the same way with the concept of 'ubiquitous home show room'. This is different from just showing home networking system in a house or in a district, it provides the functional and/or visual differentiation.

Show case suggests the change of residential concept itself rather than a future house simply listing the demonstration of items. As a space uniting and ubiquitous service items into one concept, cohesiveness of the concept has been pursued. In other words, show case that starts with a simple logic of 'residential space and ubiquitous exist for human' has differences with existing future home experience hall (exhibition) as providing house and high-technology more considered in perspectives of human.

Table 41. Experiment conditions

Condition		Details
Experience hall scale (u-Home)		Area: 125.6m^2, Room: 3 rooms.
Number of main service items		u-Home service items: 17 service items.
Sub-items	·Entrance supporting	Face recognition service, Future door, Ubiquitous Parking Information Systems (UPIS).
	·Home network control	Media table, (multimedia) Bi-directional TV, Medical camera, u-Health, Therapy music control, Lighting control, Education systems.

The experimental subject consists of a dimension of 125.6m^2 and provides seventeen ubiquitous service items. The items presented in table 41 consist of the three parts, i.e. facial recognitions for entrance, the door of future, Ubiquitous Parking Information System (UPIS), etc., media table relating to home network control, bi-directional TV relating to multi-media, medical camera relating to health, u-Health, intelligence healthy menu system, therapy music, light control, custom short message relating to living, magic mirror, digital frame, product information built-in Organic Light Emitting Diodes (OLED), Family collaborated learning system relating to education, etc. The cutting-edge equipments such as electrical sensitive toilet in one-piece with a bidet, height adjustable washstand, remote control bathtub, etc. are excluded from the experiment.

The study experiment is used to examine the metric proposed in the study and to estimate the weight (priority) for each factor. The interactivity evaluation has been performed in ubiquitous future home experience hall (h-Life exhibition hall) opened on March, 2007 (figure 20). Since the way of experiencing the ubiquitous service directly is most natural and reasonable, the detailed services of home network control, health, living or education, and safety or security are provided in differential ubiquitous future home cultural centers, which applies the latest requirements in functionality and practical use among u-Home services (h-Life, 2007). The contents of each detailed item and user task scenarios are shown in table 42 and table 43.

Figure 20. Ubiquitous experience hall (Future housing: the experimental location)

91

Table 42. Ubiquitous service component examples: u-Home service (h-Life, 2007)

Service components	Service contents	Major functions
Home network control	Air-conditioning, Ventilation, Lightning	·Sensibility mood service system of analyzing total biorhythm data and physical condition checked in bio-cognizing system, such as therapy music, digital frame, sense light, etc. ·Controlling the optimum conditions like interior light, temperature, etc. for each individual, and playing sweet therapy music to relieve fatigue of mind and body ·Control of air-conditioning, heating and gas, and supervision of trespassing ·Facial recognition: recognizes user's face before entering the front door
u-Healthcare	Healthcare service, u-Medical mirror	·Monitoring the health status with transferring data via body status check and analysis function or body scanning, and analyzing data ·Healthcare related data for user can be confirmed through the mirror in powder room, indoor temperature and light is available to adjust by checking the user's body status whenever coming back from outside ·Including the function of recommending the suitable menu for each person interlocking with u-Mom service in kitchen
u-Education	Education service	·New concept of co-study system to help homework of child at home through conversation in visual phone with one data ·Effectively use in various fields over the entire society: not only in education, but also in medical service, music composition, multi-programming, etc.
Living service	Auto kitchen	·Intelligence healthy menu, food order
	Media table	·Provide a table to talk each other in daily life, a function to confirm and control the status throughout the home, like checking visitors, etc., including electric civil affair document service to offer all sorts of civil affair documents at home

u-Magic mirror	· Provide custom information images suitable for each person as recognizing each family member · By the system controlling the home, allow user to watch the continuous images from previous watching in living room, and provide various information, such as schedule information, weather, stocks, visual phone, interphone, etc. upon requests by user
Multi-media	· The function to select bi-directional information images with recognizing the voice by promised commands in simple furniture · Digital frame provides intelligence canvas frame function, which changes to wedding picture in wedding anniversary and birthday pictures on a child's first birthday by receiving various images to keep and commemorate from integrated server

Table 43. User task scenario: u-Home service interactivity evaluation (time: minute)

Phase	Time	Space	Sub-service system	Event and/or task
1	3	Door	Home network system (Biometrics system)	· Introduction of u-Home service (pre-study) · When user enters to underground parking lot, the elevator reaches automatically, connecting to the front door by the elevator without waiting time (UPIS: Ubiquitous Parking Information Service) · Through a camera equipped at entrance, recognize the face of the entering or exiting person, if outsider, take a picture and move the data to monitoring system (if acquaintance, move to visitor album) · Recognize entering user, and confirm whether the person is the registered user or not (finger prints, facial recognition)
2	1	Door	Home network system (Short message check)	· Confirm the messages left in absence, the profile of visitor and contents of mail · Manage the daily or weekly schedule, or anniversaries
3	3	Powder room	u-Healthcare (Medical mirror)	· With medical camera attached in the left side of entrance, scan a human body in a moment and transmit the data to server · The biopsy system to check the healthy status by analyzing the data in server · Health related data for individuals can be checked through the mirror in powder room, not only indoor temperature and light is adjustable whenever coming back from outside, but also suitable menu to each person is recommended interlocking with u-Mom system in kitchen
4	1	Living room	System monitoring	· Customized sensitive mood system: analyze total body status and biorhythm data checked in biometric system, adjust indoor lights, temperature, etc., to optimal condition in for each person, and play sweet therapy music to relax fatigue of mind and body
5	5	Dress room	u-Healthcare (Magic mirror)	· System providing the best use of hours in life · Provide customized information images through the mirror as recognizing each family member · Transfer the result of body fat test to family doctor, and have remote phone conversation (IP Phone) and medical discussion · TV watched in dress room or visual phone or interphone in conversation can be connected to watch as following user's moving line (control system connected to living room, bathroom)

6	3	Bedroom 1	u-Media	· Recognize that user stops watching TV and record TV program that user has not finished · Performs functions of purchasing clothes that the characters in TV is wearing and functions in relation with health: from health information to hospital search, blood pressure and body fat measurement, health risk, health record, etc. · Digital frame: it is available to receive various images to keep and commemorate from the integrated server and change the image by anniversaries (change to wedding picture in wedding anniversary and to child's 1st birthday picture at child's birthday, etc.)
7	3	Family room	Digital media table	· Can talk each other about things in daily life through a table, confirm and control the status throughout the home, such as checking visitors, etc. (add unexpected service function: parcel delivery confirmation function) · Provide electrical civil affair document service of applying (administrative procedure) various civil affair documents at home and function of digital brochure for various living information in district, etc.
8	3	Bedroom 2	u-Education	· Bi-directional education system · New concept co-study system allowing parents in official trip and child at home to talk on the visual phone with one data and to assist homework of child
9	5	Kitchen	u-Mom	· Recognize laundry left through home network control system and inform going-out user · Listen to the relative information such as the ingredient induced in corn flake box, cookery, etc. and advertising through OLED display · With RFID, decide the necessity of foods: with order editor, order the necessary food material in the mart · Show the best menu analyzing totally various elements such as preference food, healthy status, seasonal factor, food kept in refrigerator, etc. based on provided data from biometric system, and order necessary food materials by distinguishing insufficient materials and expired foods
10	3	Living room	-	· Notify the content of service provided to user, print or transmit the desired contents · Question and answer (fully collecting the parts of short understanding or wanting to re-use) · Assessment of general satisfaction for ubiquitous service
Total	30	-	-	Executing seven spaces and ten detail events and/or tasks

95

4.3.3 Experiment method

The u-Home service has been selected to give experiences of ubiquitous service directly as a subject of interactivity assessment of ubiquitous service. Since the major subjects are u-Home service visitors and serious users, the services required in real life are constituted by user scenario.

The sequence of study experiment is experiencing event (task) of ten detail services directly in seven spaces including introduction of u-Home service, and approximately filling the questionnaires. The experiment, including the survey, takes around thirty minutes. The scenario and experience phase required to detail constituted serviced and user's experience are as figure 21 and table 43.

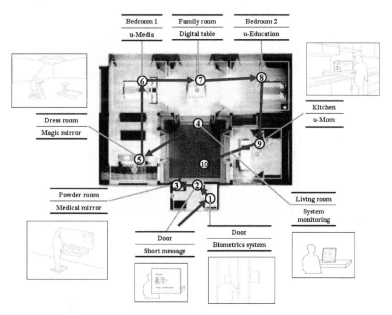

Figure 21. Experiment sequence: u-Home service (10 phase)

4.4 Result of the experiment

4.4.1 Overview of the experiment

In the experiment, investigational experiment and sensitive evaluation are executed simultaneously. Investigational experiment is executed as targeting three specific services (u-Healthcare, u-Education, u-Mom), and sensitive assessment uses within-subjects experiment plan which all of subjects assess all of services. The order of evaluation of ubiquitous service is established that the subject assesses the same task to reduce possibility of systematic error such as learning or fatigue effect.

The task used in the experiment has ten phases and the experiment is performed to the visitors for u-Home service experience. A total of a hundred and twelve people (including construction, IT service, art design, etc.) participated and a hundred and eight questionnaires were available. The survey has been executed thirty subjects per day, for four days according to the condition of experiment situation. The detailed information on the subjects is as table 44.

Table 44. Examinee technical statistic quantity

Basic data		Frequency	%
Gender	Male	59	54.1
	Female	49	45.0
Age	~20s	13	11.9
	30s	62	56.9
	40s	24	22.0
	50s ~	9	8.2
Job	IT industry	21	19.3
	Design industry	22	20.2
	Construction industry	22	20.2
	Service industry	11	10.1
	Researcher/student	16	14.6
	Homemaker etc.	16	14.6

The questionnaire contains three phrases: applicable degree evaluation of ubiquitous service constitution elements, subjective assessment of ubiquitous service user, and personal information writing, etc. To prevent a potential preconception of the examinee based on measuring values of objective measurement (design variables), the objective measurement is set to assess during an experience, and the subject assessment is to evaluate overall satisfaction after the experience. The time for evaluating one service in the experiment was limited to thirty minutes due to possible individual differences.

To measure the objective data of ubiquitous service system, service management PDA (figure 22) is used. Guided PDA provided from h-Life is used as the PDA for management. It is used for collection of objective data such as server response time, calculation of task phases required between provided services, etc.

Figure 23 is the scene of pre-evaluation orientation of ubiquitous service interactivity (left) and evaluating scene (right). The examinee has performed the objective measurement of specific services (u-Healthcare, u-Education, u-Mom) during task execution, and the subjective assessment (general satisfaction) after the use of all services.

Figure 22. PDA for evaluation used in the experiment

Figure 23. Description of experimental environment (left),
evaluation after experience (right)

4.4.2 Variable selection in u-Home service

The process of reasoning influences variable and deducing the model analyzing data gathered by interactivity evaluation of ubiquitous service is as figure 24.

First, the basic statistical characteristics which the data itself include will be analyzed through descriptive statistic analysis. In addition, the characteristics of metric are investigated based on the result of the objective and subjective evaluation. Second, using Cronbach alpha value and ANalysis Of VAriance (ANOVA), it is checked whether the data of design value and subjective measured factors gathered for interactivity evaluation, provide significant result or not. Third, by establishing design variable levels by κ-mean grouping method, it is analyzed whether each group has statistical significant influence. Fourth, the result and model of the design variable defined by using quantification I-type analysis are defined. It is figurable how each design variable level influence interactivity by analysis, and the size of influence power – between design variables which effects to interactivity as deducing partial correlation – will be established.

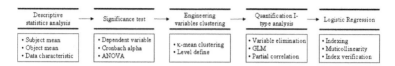

Figure 24. Analysis process of this study

Table 45. Constitution of variables

Characteristic factor			Big Y			
Measurable criteria			y_1	y_2	y_3	y_4
x_1	x_{11}, x_{12}	$u_1 \sim u_{25}$	+	+	+	
x_2	x_{21}, x_{22}	$i_1 \sim i_{10}$	+		+	
x_3	x_{31}, x_{32}	$s_1 \sim s_6$				+
x_4	x_{41}, x_{42}	$o_1 \sim o_{10}$		+		+

Constituting variables supposed in Part III can be diagramed with variables used in analysis (table 45). Fifty-one metrics are used to evaluate the relationship between ubiquitous service interactivity and service components, and to model them.

Fifty-one metrics (objective, subjective) are used to develop ubiquitous service interactivity model and calculate the priority. The variables define the relationship between four ubiquitous service characteristics and interactivity (table 46).

Table 46. Variable definition and value scale

Variable name	Variable definition	Type and level	Measurement value
Big Y	Interactivity	Quantitative, continuous data	0~100,
y_i (i=1~4)	Ubiquitous service characteristic	Quantitative, continuous data	Magnitude estimation
x_i (i=1~4)	Measurable component	Qualitative, categorical data	1~7, Likert scaling,
x_{ij} (i=1~4, j=1,2)	Measurable sub-component	Qualitative, categorical data	0~10, Numeric
u_i (i=1~25)	Measurable criteria: User	Qualitative, categorical data	data,
i_i (i=1~10)	Measurable criteria: Input artifacts	Qualitative, categorical data	Subject experiment result
s_i (i=1~6)	Measurable criteria: Service systems	Qualitative, categorical data	
o_i (i=1~10)	Measurable criteria: Output artifacts	Qualitative, categorical data	

Table 47. User experience support variable (y_1)

Metric	u_1	u_2	u_3	u_4	u_7	u_8	u_9	u_{10}	i_5	i_6	i_7	i_8	i_9	i_{10}
Mean	.875	.212	-.02	.205	.417	2.908	1.558	1.732	3.689	1.594	3.75	.169	.296	.482
Min	.467	-2.1	-2.1	0	.417	2.25	0	0	.2	.667	3.75	0	-1.9	0
Max	1	1.91	1.78	.556	.417	4.25	5	10.33	9.5	3.333	3.75	.64	2.481	1.857

Table 48. Contextualization support variable (y_2)

Metric	u_5	u_6	u_{11}	u_{12}	u_{13}	u_{14}	u_{15}	u_{16}	u_{17}	u_{18}	o_1	o_4	o_5
Mean	.146	-.13	.079	1.287	1.305	-.11	1.251	-.01	-.15	-.25	.165	.2	3.208
Min	-1.77	-2.31	0	-2.3	-1.97	-2.03	0	-2.25	-2.25	-3.67	-2.41	-1.52	3.208
Max	1.968	2.598	.32	6	6	1.572	4.667	1.92	1.929	1	1.835	1.968	3.208

Table 49. Ubiquity support variable (y_3)

Metric	u_{19}	u_{20}	u_{21}	u_{22}	u_{23}	u_{24}	u_{25}	i_1	i_2	i_3	i_4
Mean	.851	.375	.348	.441	.17	-.12	.09	.142	.418	2.25	.082
Min	.467	-1.81	-5.66	-2.08	-2.1	-5.66	-2.07	-1.91	-1.32	2.25	0
Max	1	1.984	1.939	2.215	1.872	1.642	1.929	1.742	2.21	2.25	.301

Table 50. Service capability support variable (y_4)

Metric	s_1	s_2	s_3	s_4	s_5	s_6	o_2	o_3
Mean	.081	-.78	.891	.835	-1.0	-.6	1.862	1.797
Min	0	-5.69	0	0	-5.69	-2.3	0	.333
Max	.32	1.186	2.333	1	1.346	1.967	6.667	7.333

The analyzed result of descriptive statistics for each factor defined by each ubiquitous service interactivity attribute is shown in table 47 to table 50.

Using the psychometric theory process investigated in Part II - based on the technical analysis result, sensitivity analysis is performed. To define the relationship between variables relating to ubiquitous service interactivity, the ultimate goal in the experiment, reliability analysis is referred to the result of Cronbach alpha coefficient, sensitivity analysis executes ANOVA test.

Table 51. Reliability test (Cronbach alpha)

Variable	Questionnaire	Cronbach alpha
u_1	Degree of communication direct	.771
u_2	Degree of user involvement	.770
u_3	Degree of auto control	***.701***
u_4	Degree of user effort	.763
u_5	Degree of user distance	***.706***
u_6	Degree of effectiveness	.763
u_7	Degree of efficiency	.760
u_8	Degree of response	.759
u_9	Degree of user situation	.750
u_{10}	Degree of design attraction	.751
u_{11}	Degree of multimodal interface	.766
u_{12}	Degree of one source multi use	.768
u_{13}	Degree of multi task use	.755
u_{14}	Degree of mobility	.764
u_{15}	Degree of interface touch feel, look and feel	.775

Table 51 shows the result of analyzing reliability of subjective survey variables relating to evaluation of ubiquitous service user. With reference to Cronbach alpha value, a method of reliability assessment utilized in the psychometric theory, two variables with Cronbach alpha value less than .75 have been eliminated.

Table 52. ANOVA result (α = .05, O: P $\leq$ .05)

Variable	Significance	Variable	Significance
u_1	O	i_1	O
u_4	O	i_4	O
u_8	X	i_5	O
u_9	O	i_6	O
u_{10}	O	i_8	O
u_{11}	X	i_{10}	O
u_{12}	O	o_1	O
u_{13}	X	o_2	O
u_{14}	O	o_3	O
u_{15}	O	s_1	O
u_{18}	O	s_3	X
u_{19}	X	s_4	O

Table 53. Measurement data result (time, number, etc.)

Variable	Definition	Measurement data
u_7	User recognition time before use service	O
u_{23}	Service function number using one device	O
i_3	Device sensing distance	O
i_7	Input device number during service completion	O
o_5	Loading time for specific function	O

Since the constructs are measured as multi-item or factor, the correlation is performed using singe value which is standardized and averaged from the measured terms guaranteed internal consistency by verifying reliability. The result of ANOVA test according to the objective evaluation result is as table 52.

In addition to, the variables which are processed as constant among the metrics proposed in the experiment are excluded from statistical analysis. The variables that has been referred among measuring variables and excluded from modeling are shown in table 53.

As described above, the twelve variables which are statistically meaningless in analyzing reliability and sensitivity, and defined as simple measured values, have been removed for final modeling (table 54).

The forty variables excluding twelve removed variables are used as dependent variables to establish the model. To adjust the level of meaning variables considered the sensitivity of subjects for forty variables, attributive variables are changed to each group using κ-mean clustering method. Table 55 indicates the range of groups deduced for each variable and the number of data included in each group.

Table 54. Basic statistical analysis result: removed variables

Basic statistical analysis	Removed variable
Cronbach alpha test ($\alpha < .75$)	u_3, u_5
ANOVA ($p > .05$)	$u_8, u_{11}, u_{13}, u_{19}, s_3$
Constant value	$u_7, u_{23}, i_3, i_7, o_5$

Table 55. Cluster range of the dependent variables

Var.	Cluster 1	Cluster 2	Var.	Cluster 1	Cluster 2	Var.	Cluster 1	Cluster 2
u_1	1~.875	.874~.467	u_{20}	1.984~.375	.374~-1.81	i_9	2.481~.296	.295~-1.97
u_2	1.91~.212	.211~-2.1	u_{21}	1.939~.348	.347~-5.66	i_{10}	1.481~.482	.481~0
u_4	.556~.205	.204~0	u_{22}	2.125~.441	.440~-2.08	o_1	1.835~.165	.164~-2.41
u_6	2.598~-.13	-.14~-2.31	u_{23}	1.872~.17	.16~-2.1	o_2	6.667~1.862	1.861~0
u_9	5~1.558	1.557~0	u_{24}	1.642~-.12	-.13~-5.66	o_3	7.333~1.797	1.798~.333
u_{10}	10.33~1.732	1.731~0	u_{25}	1.929~-.09	.08~-2.07	o_4	1.968~.2	.19~-1.52
u_{12}	6~1.287	1.286~-2.3	i_1	1.742~.142	.141~-1.91	s_1	.32~.081	.080~0
u_{14}	1.572~-.11	-.12~-2.03	i_2	2.21~.418	.417~-1.32	s_2	1.186~-.78	-.79~-5.69
u_{15}	4.667~1.251	1.250~0	i_4	.301~.082	.081~0	s_4	1~.835	.834~0
u_{16}	1.92~-.01	-.011~-2.25	i_5	9.5~3.689	3.688~.2	s_5	1.346~-1	-1.01~-5.69
u_{17}	1.929~-.15	-.16~-2.25	i_6	3.333~1.594	1.593~.667	s_6	1.967~-.6	-.6001~-2.3
u_{18}	1~.25	-.26~-2.25	i_8	.64~.169	.168~0			

To apply deduced groups into the model, it is needed to define the group which influences interactivity with statistical significance. Therefore, the distributed analysis for each group has been performed, indicating the statistical significance ($\alpha = .05$; $p \leq .05$). Meaning level values are used in quantification I-type analysis.

4.4.3 Quantification I-type analysis method

Quantification I-type analysis method has been analyzed with the objective measuring variable and subjective assessing variables deduced up to present as independent variables, and the characteristics of ubiquitous service interactivity as dependent variables. In addition, selecting dependent variable proposes that variables are selected based on F-value 1 of type III square sum. Therefore, the model has been formed by removing variables in the order of the experiment. These variables have the lowest values among design values in which type III square sum are less than F-value 1. Finally, considering the variables which their F-value of type III square sum are more than 1 as major influence variables, a quantification model is proposed (Hur, 1998).

The quantification I-type analysis is used to quantify the range of explanatory variate if dependent variable is quantitative and explanatory variate is qualitative (Mardia et al.,

1979; Shrestha and Kazama, 2007). The quantification I-type analysis is identified with traditional linear model (distributed analysis of unbalanced data) on external form, but quantification I-type analysis does not establish any basic statistical model while the traditional linear model is based on the typology assuming normality. There is a difference on the viewpoint of data analysis: quantification I-type analysis focuses on the quantification of each explanatory variate (i.e. deduction of each regression coefficient), while the linear model focuses on significance test of various assumptions (Tanaka et al., 1994). If quantification I-type analysis, however, is used for expectation, assuming normality of error term is unavoidable, and quantification method at that time is the same as traditional linear model method. SAS PROC GLM is used to select variables, since increasing or decreasing of explanatory power according to adding and removing explanatory variate can be known from type I square sum and type III square sum. In this case, it is reasonable to set the absolute size of F-value as default in exploratory data analysis - such as quantification I-type analysis - while statistical meaning of related partial F-value statistic (variance ratio statistic) is focused in typical ANOVA (Yeo et al., 2004).

As the factor to evaluate relative priority (contributive factor) in quantification I-type analysis, the range of quantification value or the partial correlation between quantification variables are used. In the quantification method, it re-expresses as centering as the sum of quantification values of each explanatory variate becomes 0. Therefore, the center at that time has to be a weighted average with marginal frequencies of individual category as weight. In the experiment, SAS program is used the centered quantification value in SAS output are not shown directly. The centering value is calculated by hand the range of quantification value or partial correlation between quantification values are used as the factor evaluating and comparing priority (contributive factor) of each explanatory variate. Range is the difference between maximum and minimum among quantification values within the ranges of each explanatory variate. It is considerable that explanatory variate that has a large range, contributes relatively in quantification. Partial correlation between quantification variates is used as the factor evaluating and comparing priority (contributive factor) of each explanatory variate. The reason is the partial correlation in continuous data indicates the pure linear relationship diagram between two related variates when excluding effects of the third variates.

Since the model deduced by quantification I-type analysis is a dummy variable, the influence power of each level can be known, but the influence of design variable has to be deduced by calculation. In case of range value, priorities are expressed using difference between the minimum value and the maximum value among design value levels. Partial correlation factor is the square root of the quotient of type III Square Sum (type III SS) dividing by the sum of type III square sum and error Square Sum (error SS).

Also in quantification I-type analysis, same as regression analysis, the model can be reconstituted by selecting proper variables. In consideration of quantification I-type method, however, the general method of selecting variable is not applicable because several dummy variables are required to express one categorical explanatory variable. Therefore, the method to remove the variables with F-value, by type III square sum, less than 1 is proposed (Hur, 1998). In the result of quantification I-type analysis deduced in the experiment, reconstitution has been executed continuously until deducing the model. This model finally constituted with the variables with F-values more than 1, by removing minimum design variable among the variables which F-value of type III square sum is less than 1, and executing quantification I-type analysis again.

Following quantification I-type analysis, the modeling for metric evaluation result value of interactivity factors has been executed. After modeling of user experience, contextualization, ubiquity and service capability are established. Finally, the model for interactivity of ubiquitous service has been proposed (figure 25).

106

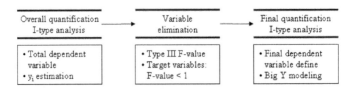

Overall quantification I-type analysis		Variable elimination		Final quantification I-type analysis

• Total dependent
  variable
• y_i estimation
		• Type III F-value
		• Target variables:
		  F-value < 1
				• Final dependent
				  variable define
				• Big Y modeling

Figure 25. Process of quantification I-type analysis method

(1) User experience support modeling: y_1

The characteristics of user experience in ubiquitous service interactivity are defined as indicated attributes in the viewpoint of service user including user preference, user involvement, etc. Modeling the user experience characteristic is executed based on characteristics factors deduced by inter-FGI, IDI process, and classified factors according to evaluating method and the relative degree. Table 56 shows type III analysis among the result of quantification I-type analysis, including the entire proposed metric variables relating to y_1.

Since the F-value of variables u_1, u_9 and i_6 are less than 1, where u_1 and u_9 have the lowest values, quantification I-type analysis without u_1 and u_9 is executed. Removing variables is performed in order of u_1, u_9, and i_6.

Table 56. Candidate variables (y_1) - Quantification I-type method: Type III analysis of effects ($R^2 = .4952$)

Variable	DF	Type III SS	F-value	Pr > F
u_1	1	12.5659	*.18*	.6777
u_2	1	186.5802	2.61	.1156
u_4	1	472.7239	6.62	.0148
u_9	1	12.6636	*.18*	.6765
u_{10}	1	517.1432	7.24	.0111
i_5	1	153.1001	2.14	.1527
i_6	1	38.9210	*.54*	.4657
i_8	1	205.0491	2.87	.0997
i_9	1	811.8500	11.36	.0019
i_{10}	1	71.3612	1.00	.3249

Table 57. Final variables (y_1) – Quantification I-type method: Type III analysis of effects ($R^2 = .4817$)

Variable	DF	Type III SS	F-value	Pr > F
u_2	1	207.4274	3.08	.0875
u_4	1	489.9413	7.29	.0105
u_{10}	1	602.7179	8.96	.0050
i_5	1	142.6533	2.12	.1539
i_8	1	216.8656	3.23	.0809
i_9	1	758.8580	11.29	.0019
i_{10}	1	35.0557	.52	.4749

After executing quantification I-type analysis three times, the result of type III error sum of deduced y_1 influence variable shows that F-value of all variables exceed 1 (table 57). Table 58 is the result of executing quantification I-type analysis consisting of meaning influential variable as independent variable and user experience as dependent variable.

In the experiment, fourteen variables are developed relating to user experience deduced by defining attributes of ubiquitous service interactivity, but it shows that seven meaning variables are deduced in the result of experiment.

Table 58. Range, centering value and partial correlation value (y_1)

Variable	Level	Centering value	Estimate	Partial correlation	Normalized value (%)
u_2*	-	-	4.6610	.281	12.3850
u_4	1	3.02683	7.0095	.410	18.0869
	2	-3.98267			
u_{10}	1	-6.46214	-9.4778	.446	19.6832
	2	3.01566			
i_5	1	-2.43441	-3.8255	.236	10.3998
	2	1.39109			
i_8	1	-3.52473	-5.1696	.287	12.6410
	2	1.64487			
i_9*	-	-	3.7448	.489	21.8369
i_{10}	1	1.18921	2.0125	.119	5.2671
	2	-.8233			

*: subjective rating variables (Likert scale)

In accordance with analysis based on centering value and estimate value, the group of 'number of user out-of-controls during service use (u_{10})' has maximum centering value and is presented as a factor to give greatest influences to user experience.

In case of variable, 'spending time to execute the input of the next service function $(i_5$: Tc – Ts, (completion time of executed specific service function) - (start time of specific service function to perform))', it is indicated that service design to reduce providing time of service result and searching time to find command function, is required.

The values of 'participation degree of bi-directional communication', 'the degree of understanding input data and expecting output at service request', or 'time rates to find the specific command function' show positive correlation (+), while 'number of user out-of-controls during service use', 'spending time to execute the input of the next service function', 'phase ratio required for requested service function', etc. show negative correlation (-). Therefore, to remove the factors interrupting user experience, controlling services controlled by user has to be available and the way to shorten executing time that reduces service executing task also has to be devised.

$$y_1 = -9.4778 \times (u_{10}) + 7.0095 \times (u_4) - 5.1696 \times (i_8) + 4.661 \times (u_2) - 3.8255 \times (i_5) + 3.7448 \times (i_9) \quad (2)$$
$$+ 2.0125 \times (i_{10}) + \text{intercept} \ (R^2 = .4817)$$

Equation (2) and table 59 are the deduced model of quantification I-type analysis results. It shows that each design variable becomes a dummy variable. The influence power for each design variable can be read into partial correlation and range values. In the estimated value and partial correlation value, they have brought somewhat different results: in the partial correlation value, the variable of 'suitable degree of system response upon service request (i_9)' has given the maximum influences.

Table 59. y_1 modeling

Variable name	Variable	Definition and level	Measurement value
y_1	User experience	·Participation or effort level of user to use the service	Magnitude estimation (0~100)
u_2	User: perception	·Participation degree for bi-directional communication, while using service	Likert scale (1~7)
u_4		·The degree of understanding input data and expecting output at service request	Metric (ratio: A/B)
u_{10}		·Number of user out-of-controls during service use	Metric (number)
i_5	Input artifacts:	·Spending time to execute input of the next service function	Metric (Tc-Ts)
i_8	service call	·Phase ratio required for requested service function	Metric (ratio: N/Tt)
i_9		·Suitable degree of system response upon service request (tedium, admittable time degree)	Likert scale (1~7)
i_{10}		·Time rates to find the specific command function	Metric (ratio: A/UOT)

These results are estimated in two kinds. First, partial correlation is the deduced result excluding effects of the third variates, the range value is calculated purely from modelers. Since tolerance square sum of the model is larger than type III square sum, in the experiment which explanatory power of data is low, the following is considered: a large difference between influences deduced by the model and the result of partial correlation deduced by tolerance. Second, deduced variable has both the objective measured variables (u_4, u_{10}, i_5, i_8, i_{10}) and subjective measured variables (u_2, i_9): the subject measured variables are impossible to calculate the range by estimating the median value. Hence it appears that there are differences on combination of partial correlations.

The quantification I-type method theory has, however, a characteristic to establish no probability model. Therefore if the relative explanation of model is required, the range value could be a more appropriate expression. To analyze the genuine effects of design variables individually, it is adequate to use partial correlation.

(2) Contextualization support modeling: y_2

Contextualization factor among the attributes of ubiquitous service interactivity is a factor that highlights the attributes of 'ubiquitous service' itself rather than other three factors. It is a service attribute factor directing sensor network and intelligence service representative with context-awareness. Contextualization characteristics modeling has been executed in the basis of factor distinguished by relative degrees with assessment, and characteristic factor deduced through FGI and IDI progress. Table 60 shows the sum of type III errors among the result of quantification I-type analysis including entire proposed metric variables relating to y_2.

The F-value of variables u_6, u_{14}, u_{16}, u_{17} and o_4 are less than 1. Quantification I-type analysis, removing u_6 to indicate it as the minimum value, is executed. Removing meaningless variables is processed in order of u_6, u_{16}, u_{17}, u_{14}, and o_4.

After executing quantification I-type analysis four times, the result of type III error sum of deduced y_2 influence variable shows that F-value of all variables exceed 1 (table 61).

Table 60. Candidate variables (y_2) - Quantification I-type method: Type III analysis of effects ($R^2 = .4501$)

Variable	DF	Type III SS	F-value	Pr > F
u_6	1	.4490	*.00*	.9548
u_{12}	1	505.7988	3.67	.0646
u_{14}	1	75.0663	*.54*	.4660
u_{15}	1	216.9635	1.57	.2189
u_{16}	1	5.2691	*.04*	.8462
u_{17}	1	35.4983	*.26*	.6153
o_1	1	271.8894	1.97	.1700
o_4	1	130.1711	*.94*	.3386

111

Table 61. Final variables (y_2) - Quantification I-type method: Type III analysis of effects (R^2 = .4321)

Variable	DF	Type III SS	F-value	Pr > F
u_{12}	1	494.0960	3.95	.0546
u_{15}	1	227.3767	1.82	.1860
o_1	1	419.3134	3.36	.0755
o_4	1	175.8802	1.41	.2435

Table 62. Range, centering value and partial correlation value (y_2)

Variable	Level	Centering value	Estimate	Partial correlation	Normalized value (%)
u_{12}*	-	-	7.133	.319	30.83
u_{15}	1	-3.1818	-5.091	.222	21.51
	2	1.9091			
o_1	1	2.7376	6.844	.296	28.62
	2	-4.1064			
o_4*	-	-	6.672	.197	19.03

*: subjective rating variables (Likert scale)

In the experiment, fourteen variables are developed relating to contextualization deduced by defining attributes of ubiquitous service interactivity, but it shows that four meaning variables are deduced in the result of experiment. In accordance with the analysis based on the centering value and estimate value, the group of 'required time and/or degree for user to modify the service function procedure in user's convenience (u_{12})' has the maximum centering value and is presented as a factor giving greatest influences to contextualization (table 62).

The variable 'ratio of error occurrence during service use (u_{15}: A/B, (number of service error)/(number of executing service))' shows its influence on the characteristics of contextualization as the lowest among others. The variables of 'required time or degree for user to modify the service function procedure in user's convenience', 'suitability degree of service feedback felt by user', and 'instinctive understandability degree of the service function result' show correlation (+), while the variable of 'ratio of error occurrence during service use' shows correlation (-) with one another. As the result of the experiment, the ratio of error occurrence is shown as $0 \sim 4.6$ points, showing that using output responses is depended on the execution of total of three sub-service tasks (u-Mom, u-Education, u-Healthcare).

$$y_2 = 7.1332 \times (u_{12}) + 6.844 \times (o_1) + 6.6727 \times (o_4) - 5.091 \times (u_{15}) + \text{intercept } (R^2 = .4321) \qquad (3)$$

Equation (3) and table 63 are the deduced model of results of quantification I-type analysis. The estimate value and partial correlation value have brought somewhat different results: in both the estimate value and partial correlation value, the variable 'required time or degree for user to modify the service function procedure in user's convenience (u_{12})' indicates to give the largest influences. The important value proposed in both methods is 'suitability degree of service feedback felt by user (o_4)'. This is a barometer deciding how the result of user's required service is provided properly and appropriately to fit in the situation, and it is decided as the representative variable of contextualization attributes.

The reason of these results is: the deduced variables have both objective measured variables (u_{15}, o_1) and subjective measured variables (u_{12}, o_4). Since it is impossible to calculate the range assuming median value of subjective measured variable, it can be shown that there is a difference between mixing partial correlations.

Table 63. y_2 modeling

Variable name	Variable	Definition and level	Measurement value
y_2	Contextualization	· Provides services adequate to the situation, considered the relation of service and user	Magnitude estimation (0~100)
u_{12}	User: perception	· Required time or degree for user to modify the service function procedure in user's convenience	Likert scale (1~7)
u_{15}		· Ratio of error occurrence during service use	Metric (ratio: A/B)
o_1	Output artifacts (multimedia):	· Instinctive understandability degree of the service function result	Metric (number)
o_4	browsing/ execution	· Suitability degree of service feedback felt by user	Likert scale (1~7)

(3) Ubiquity support modeling: y_3

The characteristics of ubiquity in ubiquitous service interactivity, is defined as indicated attributes in the viewpoint of service user including mobility, portability, etc. Ubiquity characteristic modeling has been executed in the basis of indicator distinguished by relative degrees with assessment and characteristic indicator deduced through FGI and IDI progress.

Table 64 shows the sum of type III errors among the result of quantification I-type analysis including the entire proposed metric variables relating to y_3.

The F-value of variables u_{20}, u_{21}, u_{22}, u_{23}, u_{24} and u_{25} are less than 1, thus quantification I-type analysis removing u_{24} indicating as the minimum value is executed. Removing variables is performed in order of u_{24}, u_{25}, u_{23}, u_{22}, u_{21}, and u_{20}.

After executing quantification I-type analysis three times, the result of type III error sum of deduced y_3 influence variable shows that F-value of all variables exceed 1 (table 65).

Table 64. Candidate variables (y_3) - Quantification I-type method: Type III analysis of effects ($R^2 = .4151$)

Variable	DF	Type III SS	F-value	Pr > F
u_{20}	1	236.0724	.96	.3353
u_{21}	1	175.5672	.71	.4051
u_{22}	1	167.5456	.68	.4159
u_{23}	1	56.2468	.23	.6362
u_{24}	1	3.6098	.01	.9045
u_{25}	1	47.4752	.19	.6638
i_1	1	761.4278	.09	.0885
i_2	1	512.2920	.08	.1593
i_4	1	785.6161	.19	.0838

114

Table 65. Final variables (y_3) - Quantification I-type method: Type III analysis of effects (R^2 = .4009)

Variable	DF	Type III SS	F-value	Pr > F
u_{20}	1	237.9405	1.03	.3163
u_{21}	1	233.3203	1.01	.4059
u_{22}	1	233.0892	1.01	.4831
i_1	1	1080.4595	4.69	.0372
i_2	1	664.7439	2.89	.0981
i_4	1	1308.0350	5.68	.0227

Table 66. Range, centering value and partial correlation value (y_3)

Variable	Level	Centering value	Estimate	Partial correlation	Normalized value (%)
u_{20}^{*}	-	-	9.3021	.169	11.90
u_{21}^{*}	-	-	12.8308	.141	9.89
u_{22}^{*}	-	-	12.3577	.119	8.36
i_1	1	4.3105	10.6495	.344	24.16
	2	-6.3389			
i_2^{*}	-	-	11.6151	.276	19.40
i_4	1	-5.6971	-12.5936	.374	26.27
	2	6.8964			

*: subjective rating variables (Likert scale)

In the experiment, eleven variables are developed relating to ubiquity deduced by defining attributes of ubiquitous service interactivity, but it shows six meaning variables deduced in the result of experiment (table 66). In accordance with the analysis based on the centering value and estimate value, the group of 'at request of specific service function, modifiable degree with various devices (i_4)' has the maximum centering value and is presented as a factor to give greatest influences to ubiquity ((number of reduced steps to execute the function after modifying the service function)/(number of steps to execute the function before modifying the service function)).

Among ubiquity characteristics, a variable indicating 'application degree of visual or voice interface' deems to highlight the significance of multimodal interface. Most of all variables show correlation (+) and the most powerful influence variables are indicated by the method of usable input device. Also the factor which decides 'usable input method or various interactivity degrees (i_1)' indicates various interactivity degrees. The result of the experiment is evaluated between 1.7 and 1.9, which shows that multimodal interfaces that are less than 2 and are provided to assist service practical use of user.

$$y_3 = 12.8308 \times (u_{21}) - 12.5936 \times (i_4) + 12.3577 \times (u_{22}) + 11.6151 \times (i_2) + 10.6495 \times (i_1) \qquad (4)$$
$$+ 9.3021 \times (u_{20}) + \text{intercept} \ (R^2 = .4009)$$

Equation (4) and table 67 are the deduced model of result of quantification I-type analysis. In estimate value and partial correlation value, they have brought somewhat different results: in both of the estimate value and partial correlation value, the influence degree of 'design suitability of input devices (u_{20})', 'suitability of weight and size of input devices (u_{21})' which are variables in relation with user's input use has presented to be little high.

The same point of values indicated in both of methods is: ubiquity attribute of ubiquitous service interactivity shows the importance of applying multimodal interface.

Table 67. y_3 modeling attributes

Variable name	Variable	Definition and level	Measurement value
y_3	Ubiquity	·Portability and pervasive connectedness	Magnitude estimation (0~100)
u_{20}	User: manipulation	·Design suitability of input devices (look & feel degree)	Likert scale (1~7)
u_{21}		·Suitability of weight and size of input devices	Likert scale (1~7)
u_{22}		·Application degree of visual or voice interface	Likert scale (1~7)
i_1	Input artifacts: recognition	·Usable input method or various interactivity degrees (keyboards, stylus pen, audio input, touch screen etc.)	Metric (number)
i_2		·Usable degree of multimodal devices same service functions	Likert scale (1~7)
i_4		·At request of specific service function, modifiable degree with various devices (touch screen-remote control)	Metric (ratio: A/B)

Application degree of multimodal interface means the input devices use applicable at anywhere for the interactivity without bottleneck situation in a position of user receiving ubiquitous service. For that reason, single modality has weakness of lacking reliability and accuracy (Cohen et al., 1998). By providing a service integrated with various human senses for convenient use of the service in anywhere, it could facilitate the interactivity between service and the user.

Also from the calculated result of ubiquity attribute priority, abstracted six variables are consisted with four subjective variables and two objective measured variables: the subject measured variables are impossible to calculate the range by estimating the median value, hence it appears to be that there are differences on combination of partial correlation.

(4) Service capability support modeling: y_4

The one of differential characteristics of ubiquitous service from typical personal service is that the performance viewpoint of service system is included. In the experiment, the viewpoint of service user is defined as defining interactivity attribute as service capability. Service capability characteristic modeling has been executed in the basis of indicator distinguished by relative degrees with assessment and characteristic indicator deduced through FGI and IDI progress. Table 68 shows the sum of type III error among the result of quantification I-type analysis included entire proposed metric variables relating to y_4.

Table 68. Candidate variables (y_4) - Quantification I-type method: Type III analysis of effects ($R^2 = .4740$)

Variable	DF	Type III SS	F-value	Pr > F
s_1	1	100.5715	1.15	.2911
s_2	1	66.4857	.76	.3895
s_4	1	93.7476	1.07	.3078
s_5	1	67.8128	.77	.3848
s_6	1	5.5543	*.06*	.8027
o_2	1	1.7553	*.02*	.8883
o_3	1	60.9579	.69	.4097

Table 69. Final variables (y_4) - Quantification I-type method: Type III analysis of effects ($R^2 = .4722$)

Variable	DF	Type III SS	F-value	Pr > F
s_1	1	104.1280	1.25	.2624
s_2	1	86.3097	1.03	.3428
s_4	1	107.9256	1.29	.2624
s_5	1	84.6338	1.01	.3962
o_3	1	88.8236	1.06	.3086

Table 70. Range, centering value and partial correlation value (y_4)

Variable	Level	Centering value	Estimate	Partial correlation	Normalized value (%)
s_1	1	-2.7006	-3.7615	.174	20.2136
	2	1.0609			
s_2^*	-	-	5.6966	.150	18.8515
s_4	1	-1.0888	-3.5385	.177	22.2196
	2	2.4497			
s_5^*	-	-	7.7758	.134	16.8783
o_3	1	-2.4054	-3.4745	.161	20.2136
	2	1.0691			

*: subjective rating variables (Likert scaling)

Since the F-value of variables s_2, s_5, s_6, o_2 and o_3 are less than 1, where o_2 has the minimum value, quantification I-type analysis removing o_2 is executed. Removing variables is performed in order of o_2, s_6, o_3, s_2, and s_5. After executing quantification I-type analysis twice, the result of type III error sum of deduced y_4 influence variable shows that F-value of all variables exceeds 1 (table 69).

In the experiment, twelve variables are developed relating to service capability deduced by defining attribute of ubiquitous service interactivity, but five meaning variables are deduced shown in the result of experiment (table 70). In accordance with analyses based on centering value and estimate value, the group of 'suitability of temporary storage saving to provide requested function (s_5)' has the maximum centering value and is presented as a factor to give greatest influences to service capability.

'Suitability ratio of service functions (s_1: A/B, (number of ubiquitous service functions occurred error)/(total number of ubiquitous service functions))', 'stability degree of service system when adding/removing a service function', etc. are indicated as the parts considered especially in service system capability.

The variables of 'data adjustable degree between service in operating and the component of other services (s_2)' and 'suitability of temporary storage saving to provide requested function (s_5)' show strong correlation (+). The value relating to 'number of requesting help to confirm the specific output device result (o_3)' is indicated with a proper range, .3~1.8, of the evaluated service system (u-Mom, u-Healthcare, u-Education).

In case of u-Education service system, events of expanding service functions with additional HW/SW have been examined, the average result indicates positive value, and it could be analogized that the extensive service function works as a cause to improve interactivity of ubiquitous service user.

$$y_4 = 7.7758 \times (s_5) + 5.6966 \times (s_2) - 3.7615 \times (s_1) - 3.5385 \times (s_4) - 3.4745 \times (o_3) + \text{intercept} \qquad (5)$$

$$(R^2=.4722)$$

Table 71. y_4 modeling attributes

Variable name	Variable	Definition and level	Measurement value
y_4	Service capability	· Level of user protection and error prevention at service	Magnitude estimation (0~100)
s_1	Service system: integration	· Suitability ratio of service functions	Metric (ratio: A/B)
s_2		· Data adjustable degree between service in operating and the component of other services	Likert scale (1~7)
s_4	Service system: capsulation	· Stability degree of service system when adding or removing a service function	Metric (ratio: 1-A/B)
s_5		· Suitability of temporary storage saving to requested function	Likert scale (1~7)
o_3	Output artifacts (multimedia): browsing/execution	· Number of requesting help to confirm the specific output device result	Metric (number)

119

Equation (5) and table 71 are the model deduced from the result of quantification I-type analysis. It shows that each design variable becomes a dummy variable. The influence power for each design variable can be read into partial correlation and range value. A different result has been presented in estimate value and partial correlation value. In partial correlation value, it is presented that the variable 'stability degree of service system when adding or removing a service function (s_4)' experimented in specific service (u-Education) gives the greatest influences.

The reason of obtaining these results is: partial correlation is the deduced result excluding the all of effects of third variates and the range value is calculated purely from modelers. Since the tolerance square sum of the model is more than the type III square sum in the experiment which explanatory power of data is low, it is considered that there is a difference between influences deduced by the model. The result of partial correlation was deduced by tolerance ranges.

(5) Interactivity support modeling: Big Y

To deduce the final model relating to ubiquitous service interactivity, Big Y (interactivity) modeling which has y_1, y_2, y_3 and y_4 values as independent variable, is executed. A small y value used as dependent variable is input as a continuous value. The interactivity modeling has been executed using multiple regression analysis module of SAS 8.0 'e-Miner' (R^2=0.7040). From the multiple regression results, with R^2 (coefficient of determination) 70.4%, F-value (model fitness) 60.66, p-value .0001 (<.05), the proposed model is approved to be significant (table 72; table 73).

Table 72. ANOVA result (Big Y)

Source	DF	Sum of squares	Mean square	F-value	Pr>F
Model	4	10201	2550.2333	60.66	<.0001
Error	102	4288.2629	42.0418		
Corrected total	106	14489			

Table 73. Analysis of maximum likelihood estimates (Big Y)

Parameter	DF	Estimate	Standard error	t-value	Pr > |t|
Intercept	1	13.1316	4.5690	2.87	.0049
y_1	1	.3044	.1036	2.94	.0041
y_2	1	.3694	.1174	3.15	.0022
y_3	1	.0978	.0873	1.12	.0265
y_4	1	.2597	.0900	2.89	.0048

Estimated factors are significant as each t-value is 2.87, 2.94, 3.15, 1.12 and 2.89. All of t-probability appears to have meaning, but for y_3, which gives a result with comparatively low values than other variables (.0265). As both dependent variable and independent variable are continuous variables, the model satisfied with ubiquitous service interactivity-satisfaction can be expressed as equation with estimate value.

$$\text{Big Y} = .3694 \times (y_2) + .3044 \times (y_1) + .2597 \times (y_4) + .0978 \times (y_3) + \text{intercept. } (R^2 = .7040) \qquad (6)$$

Equation (6) and table 74 are the models deduced from the result of multiple regression analysis. As resulted from modeling with estimate value, the killer attributes of ubiquitous service interactivity appear to be contextualization support attributes, and the influence degrees are presented in the order of user experience support, service capability support and ubiquity support.

Table 74. Big Y modeling

Variable name	Variable	Definition	Measurement value
Big Y	Interactivity	· Degree of level of ubiquitous service interactivity	Magnitude estimation (0~100)
y_1	User experience	· Degree of level of user involvement and effort	Magnitude estimation (0~100)
y_2	Contextualization	· Degree of supporting of context-awareness between service systems and users	Magnitude estimation (0~100)
y_3	Ubiquity	· Degree of unobtrusiveness of mobility and connectivity	Magnitude estimation (0~100)
y_4	Service capability	· Degree of error protection level of service user	Magnitude estimation (0~100)

The initial constitution concept of ubiquitous service means the network service connected everywhere. In the viewpoint of providing custom service recognizing user's situation as the number of users grow (John et al., 2007), the interactivity model is assumed that the characteristics of contextualization, as well as the user experience support are meaning influence factors in interactivity. Service capability support is an attribute specified for ubiquitous service environment that cannot be recognized in the existing personal service, and it has been acknowledged that it plays a significant role to improve the performance of back-end for interactivity advancement of ubiquitous service user. For ubiquity support, meaning the conceptual characteristic of 'ubiquitous', however it has been concluded as a attribute on the extension of web service and mobile service, so that it is somewhat difficult to interpret as a variable to explain the breakthrough of paradigm for ubiquitous service interactivity.

Figure 26 and table 75 are the calculated result of priority for each factor deduced from the experimental result. From the result, factors with different priority of each dependent variable are deduced, and estimate value of each explanatory variable is changed to normalized-value. The integrated modeling result indicates that the most significant variable among interactivity attributes of ubiquitous service is the contextualization support attributes, and it presents that 'perception: time ratio (correcting time for service procedure)' metric has the highest priority as a dependent variable, and on the contrary, 'perception: user control level using service manipulation' metric is a dependent variable containing most negative influences.

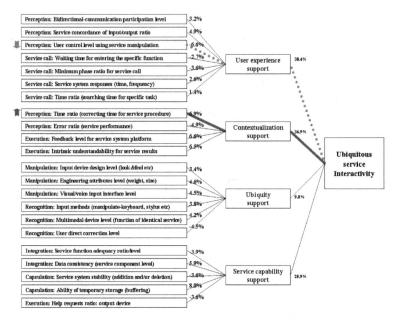

Perception: Bidirectional-communication participation level	3.2%
Perception: Service concordance of input/output ratio	4.9%
Perception: User control level using service manipulation	5.6%
Service call: Waiting time for entering the specific function	-2.7%
Service call: Minimum phase ratio for service call	-3.6%
Service call: Service system responses (time, frequency)	2.6%
Service call: Time ratio (searching time for specific task)	1.4%
Perception: Time ratio (correcting time for service procedure)	4.9%
Perception: Error ratio (service performance)	-4.9%
Execution: Feedback level for service system platform	6.6%
Execution: Intrinsic understandability for service results	6.5%
Manipulation: Input device design level (look &feel etc)	3.4%
Manipulation: Engineering attributes level (weight, size)	4.6%
Manipulation: Visual/voice input interface level	4.5%
Recognition: Input methods (manipulate-keyboard, stylus etc)	3.8%
Recognition: Multimodal device level (function of identical service)	4.2%
Recognition: User direct correction level	-4.5%
Integration: Service function adequacy ratio/level	3.9%
Integration: Data consistency (service component level)	5.0%
Capsulation: Service system stability (addition and/or deletion)	-3.6%
Capsulation: Ability of temporary storage (buffering)	8.0%
Execution: Help requests ratio: output device	3.6%

User experience support — 38.4%

Contextualization support — 36.9%

Ubiquity support — 9.8%

Service capability support — 25.9%

Ubiquitous service Interactivity

Figure 26. Structural interactivity model using selected indicators

123

Table 75. Interactivity indicators to evaluate ubiquitous service

(O: Objective, S: Subjective)

		Ubiquitous service characteristic factor	y_1 (user experience)	y_2 (contextualization)	y_3 (ubiquity)	y_4 (service capability)
		Measurable criteria				
u-Service user	Perception	· Participation degree of bi-directional communication, while using service	S	-	-	-
		· The degree of understanding input data and expecting output at service request	S/O	-	-	-
		· Number of user out-of-controls during service use	O	-	-	-
		· Required time or degree for user to modify the service function procedure in user's convenience	-	S/O	-	-
		· Ratio of error occurrence during service use	-	O	-	-
	Manipulation	· Design suitability of input devices (look & feel degree)	-	-	S	-
		· Suitability of weight and size of input devices	-	-	S	-
		· Application degree of visual or voice interface	-	-	S	-
u-Service input artifacts (sensor, actuator)	Recognition	· Usable input method or various interactivity degrees (keyboard, stylus, etc.)	-	-	S/O	-
		· Usable degree of multimodal devices same service functions	-	-	S	-
		· At request of specific service function, modifiable degree with various devices (e.g.: touch screen vs. remote control)	-	-	S/O	-
	Service call	· Spending time to execute the input of the next service function	S/O	-	-	-
		· Phase ratio required for requested service function	O	-	-	-
		· Suitable degree of system response upon service request (tedium, admittable time degree)	S	-	-	-
		· Time rates to find the specific command function	O	-	-	-

u-Service systems	Integration	· Suitability ratio of service functions: number of problem occurrence or number of total functions	-	-	-	O
		· Data adjustable degree between service in operating and the component of other services	-	-	-	S
	Capsulation	· Stability degree of service system when adding or removing a service function	-	-	-	O
		· Suitability of temporary storage saving to provide requested function (buffering degree)	-	-	-	S
u-Service Output artifacts (multi-media)	Browsing & Execution	· Number of requesting help to confirm the specific output device result	-	-	-	O
		· Suitability degree of service feedback felt by user	-	S	-	-
		· Instinctive understandability degree of the service function result	-	S	-	-

4.4.4 Interactivity and user satisfaction model index

(1) Overview

The statistical analysis method used in this study was the quantification I-type analysis method for the construction of subjective assessment variable and design variable of user. The regression analysis was also used for the final modeling.

As the metric developed for the user's research and the evaluation variables are theoretically expected to have some relations, the indicators on the use of ubiquitous service can be suggested through the interactivity evaluation variables. First, an appropriate model is suggested out of the quantification I-type analysis method, and then the interactivity indicators for the ubiquitous service can be calculated on the basis of the model.

The interactivity model was constructed to make out the interactivity of the ubiquitous service through the distinctive sub-variables and finally to predict the satisfaction. At the stage of the development of ubiquitous service, a scenario on the diverse future services is made and used. According to the research agents, different scenarios are made in consideration of the project reality and the duplication of development goals. In the level of scenario technology, the accumulation of many researches has enabled to provide the refined scenarios reflecting the reality better (SAIT, 2005). When considering the current situation with many technological and economical restrictions in realization of the ubiquitous services, the evaluation method of scenario may be the best alternative. In addition to the refined technologies on the future services, we need the appropriate evaluation system centered on the users with the peculiarity of ubiquitous service in contents. Therefore, as a conclusion of this study, we are going to suggest an interactivity index for the ubiquitous service that can evaluate it in the practical affairs on the basis of the interactivity-satisfaction model.

Here the Logistic Regression (LR), which is comparatively better in the performance of classification techniques, is used. LR, a categorical response analysis model, is a special form of regression analysis. In producing procedure of the indicator for this study, LR is suitable in the following reasons:

First, in case of the independent variables exceeding the interval scale and the variables are in the multivariate normal distribution: the discriminant analysis is used in general. But, when the independent variables are mixed in the qualitative scale, and the interval scale and the hypothesis is not clear that the variables are in the multivariate normal distribution, LR is preferable to use. As the quantification I-type analysis does not require the normal distribution, LR is appropriate for the development of indicator through the quantification I-type analysis (Mojsilovic et al., 2007). There is another advantage that it can be used in the situation that the normal scales such as nominal, ordinal scale and the interval scale are mixed for the independent variables, and they may not be in the multivariate normal distribution.

Second, in LR, the choice probability has the form of logistic function and the interpretation on a population parameter is made under the supposition that the other expositive variable factors are restricted or fixed. It has the same philosophical approach as the quantification analysis in finding out which variable is more important in the group-classifying formula and in classifying the groups in each sample for samples from more than two groups. Thus, it is very appropriate for producing the index.

Third, according to diverse studies (Moisen and Frescino, 2002; Delen et al., 2004; Kurt et al., 2007), the performance of LR is proved to be superior to that of other similar methods such as Classification And Regression Tree (CART), Multi-Layer Perception (MLP), Self-Organizing Feature Maps (SOFM). Thus, it is used for the index development in this study. This study used twenty-two metrics derived through the quantification I-type analysis method for the index development.

(2) Indicator development

LR is a model to estimate the probability $\hat{p}$ that a ubiquitous service shows the interactivity disposition through a given expositive variable x. For the development of indicators, we used SAS 8.0 Logistic Regression module. To realize the logistic multiple regression model with two or more expositive variable factors, we carried out the indicator development for the twenty-two metrics derived from the quantification I-type analysis. The logistic multiple regression model is described as in equation (7).

$$\log it = \beta_0 + \beta_1 x_1 + \beta x_2 + \ldots + \beta_n x_n \tag{7}$$

In the category that was cross-classified by all expositive variable factors, p represents the ratio of the case that the response variable Y=1. The coefficient β_n in the model represents the effect of corresponding expositive variable for the logit when all other expositive variables are fixed (Jo, 2004). Table 76 shows the statistic values of the results predicted by the significance degree and population estimate of the model.

In the Akaike Information Criterion (AIC) value and Schwartz Criterion (SC) value showing the significance degree of the present model, the value of the intercept and covariance becomes less than values of the intercept only, and the value of -2 log L also has the same tendency. The χ^2 of the variables was also very significant (χ^2=61.1204).
For the analysis of variables, twenty-two metrics significantly derived from the quantification I-type analysis were provided as the independent variables. Then, based on the p-value of .2, the final candidate variable was derived through the stepwise method (table 77).

Table 76. Model fit statistics

Criterion	Intercept only	Intercept and Covariates
AIC	65.683	22.562
SC	67.511	40.849
-2 Log L	63.683	2.562

Table 77. Summary of stepwise selection

| Step | Effect | | DF | Number in | Chi-square | | Pr > ChiSq |
	Entered	Removed			Score	Wald	
1	o_4		1	1	5.8131		.0159
2	i_5		1	2	6.1959		.0128
3	u_{10}		1	3	6.4614		.0110
4	i_{10}		1	4	3.9454		.0470
5	u_{15}		1	5	3.5331		.0602
6	u_{16}		1	6	1.7253		.1890
7	i_2		1	7	2.6191		.1056
8	s_5		1	8	2.5643		.1043
9	u_4		1	9	1.9083		.1672
10		u_{16}	1	8		.7385	.3902
11	u_{21}		1	9	1.8759		.1708
12	u_{25}		1	10	1.3729		.2413
13		u_{25}	1			.4502	.5022

Table 78 is the result for the regression coefficient β_n. When the interactivity attributions are classified into the function-based, cognition-based, and activity-based according to the Y value, we can decide which category the corresponding service goes into through the result of logistic regression analysis.

The estimated value in the above table is for β_n, which also works as the coefficient of equation (8) (log*it* function).

Table 78. Analysis of maximum likelihood estimates

Variable	DF	Estimate	Standard error	Wald Chi-Square	Pr > ChiSq
Intercept 1	1	9.3032	3.7008	6.3193	.0119
Intercept 2	1	.7419	2.6152	.0805	.7767
u_{10}	1	-2.9867	1.7597	2.8808	.0896
u_{21}	1	2.8698	2.1984	1.7041	.1918
i_5	1	-8.9299	3.5117	6.4663	.0110
s_5	1	1.9163	1.2286	2.4325	.1188
u_4	1	2.0151	1.2835	2.4647	.1164
i_{10}	1	-1.0304	.5631	3.3487	.0673
o_4	1	1.9481	.7225	7.2698	.0070
i_2	1	.7559	.5272	2.0556	.1516
u_{15}	1	-1.3265	.6751	3.8603	.0494

$$\log it = \ln(\frac{\hat{Y}}{1-\hat{Y}}) = \beta_0 + \beta_1 x_1 + \beta x_2 + \ldots + \beta_n x_n \qquad (8)$$

By calculating $\hat{Y}$, we can decide which category is appropriate (equation (9)).

$$\hat{Y} = \frac{1}{1 + e^{-(\beta_0 + \beta_1 x_1 + \beta x_2 + \ldots + \beta_n x_n)}} \qquad (9)$$

If infer the index model in consideration of the relation with the probability, we can see that the formula to get the logit value through the results must be equation (10) (estimate Y).

$$\log it = 9.3032 + .7419 - 8.9299 \times (i_5) - 2.9867 \times (u_{10}) + 2.8698 \times (u_{21}) + 2.0151 \times (u_4)$$
$$+ 1.9481 \times (o_4) + 1.9163 \times (s_5) - 1.3265 \times (u_{15}) - 1.0304 \times (i_{10}) + 0.7559 \times (i_2) \qquad (10)$$

For example, if (i_5) value increases by 1, the logit of Y is predicted to decrease at the rate of 8.9299. By the way, as the meaning of logit is abstract, it is more useful to interpret the meaning of population estimates as that of *odds* rather than logit concept (Kim, 2004). Therefore, the index model of the result was described with the *odds* concept as shown in equation (11) (transformed *odds* formula).

$$odds = \frac{\hat{Y}}{1-\hat{Y}} = e^{(\beta_0 + \beta_1 x_1 + \beta x_2 + \ldots + \beta_n x_n)} \qquad (11)$$

It can be interpreted that β_n of LR is expected to change by e^{β_n} times in *odds* when x_n changes by a unit. The change of *odds* according to the change of each variable is shown in table 79. If (u_{10}) value increases by 1, the *odds* value decreases by .050 times, and if (s_5) value increases by 1, the *odds* value increases by 6.796 times equation (12).

$$odds = e^{(9.303+.742-8.93\times(i_5)-2.987\times(u_{10})+2.87\times(u_{21})+2.015\times(u_4)+1.948\times(o_4)+1.916\times(s_5)-1.327\times(u_{15})-1.03\times(i_{10})+.756\times(i_2))}$$

(12)

Table 79. *Odds* ratio estimates

Effect	Point estimate	95% Wald confidence
u_{10}	.050	.002
u_{21}	17.634	.024
i_5	<.001	<.001
s_5	6.796	.612
u_4	.133	.011
i_{10}	.127	.014
o_4	49.215	2.898
i_2	4.535	.574
u_{15}	.070	.005

β_n of LR represents the rate of change of predicted probability p that changes according to the x-value. Positive or (+) means the increase, and negative or (-) means the decrease.

Table 80 shows the rate of expected results. In the result, we can see that the rate of correct prediction by the current model is 94.2% and the incorrect rate is 5.6%. The Somer's D, Gamma Tau-a, and c represent the correlations with the ordinal statistic quantities. As all the values are close to 1 and positive, the prediction can be said to be well-developed.

(3) Verification of Estimated Index

The verification of estimated index can be made in two points of view. The first is the null hypothesis verification that decides whether they have the prediction ability for the probability p of expositive variable.

Table 80. Association of predicted probabilities and observed responses

% concordant	94.2	Somers' D	.887
% discordant	5.6	Gamma	.888
% tied	.2	Tau-a	.446
Pairs	521	c	.943

The second is the goodness-of-fit verification that decides how well the suggested model is fit for the given data (Agresti, 1996). In this study, the variables have not been derived from the raw data but suggested by application of deduced variables through the quantification I-type analysis. Therefore, we verified the index through the goodness-of-fit analysis between the expected frequency and the observed frequency rather than the omnibus test for model coefficients.

The estimated logistic regressive model can be used to predict the probability p of reaction when a certain expositive variable value is given, or to acquire the value of expositive variable that predicts a certain probability p (Park, 2006). The value of expositive variable that predict the specific reaction probability $p=.5$ is called 'median effective level', and indicated by EL_{50}. The median effective level EL_{50} is considered as a kind of 'threshold'. If the value is more than EL_{50}, it is interpreted as y. As $EL_{50}=-b_0/\sum b_n$, and if b_n is very large, it means that the threshold of the reaction is very low. Therefore, it means that a small occurrence of the expositive variable represented by the sensitivity can bring out the y reaction.

If the model suggested by equation (12) is correct, the population estimate of rate of error occurrence during the service (u_{15}), for example, will be as high as $e^{-1.3265} = .2654$ times when the other variables are the results of the same service. The influence of each expositive variable using *odds* is shown in table 81.

Table 81. Factor loading by using *Odds* value

Effect	Odds	Priority
u_{21}	$e^{2.8698}$	17.6334
u_4	$e^{2.0151}$	7.5015
s_5	$e^{1.9163}$	6.7958
o_4	$e^{1.481}$	4.3973
u_{15}	$e^{1.3265}$	3.7678
i_2	$e^{0.7559}$	2.1295
u_{10}	$e^{-2.9867}$	.0504
i_{10}	$e^{-1.0304}$	.0359
i_5	$e^{-8.9299}$	.0001

To verify the result of logistic regression analysis, we have analyzed the goodness-of-fit with the real data. We checked how close the Big Y value predicted through the result is to the real Big Y value, and tested how appropriate the suggested index is.

We defined three intervals through the frequency analysis of Big Y. The three intervals were named as 'function-based', 'cognition-based', and 'activity-based' according to the mature level of interactivity (Heeter, 2000; Dag et al., 2001; Hammer and Reichl, 2005).

The intervals of suggested level were defined as 0~70 points (level 1), 71~85 points (level 2), and 86~100 points (level 3) according to the saturation point value of frequency (Diggle et al., 2002; figure 27).

The prediction of estimate Big Y interval was classified into 0~.48, .49~.999, .999 < as level 1, level 2 and level 3 respectively on the basis of .48. The median effective level (threshold point) is shown below in table 82.

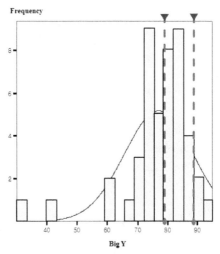

Figure 27. Frequency histogram for Big Y result (3-layer)

Table 82. Define levels of an index test

Level	User data (0~100 points)	Estimate Big Y (threshold points)
Level 1	0~70 points	< .48
Level 2	71~85 points	.49 ~ .999
Level 3	86~100 points	.999 <

Table 83. Example: Interactivity index validation test

User	Estimate	i_5	u_{10}	u_{21}	u_4	o_4	u_{15}	i_{10}	i_2	s_5	$\beta_n x_n$	$\hat{Y}$
1	9.3	.74	-9	-3	2.9	-2	1.3	1.3	-1	.5	.6	-8	.0005
2	9.3	.74	-9	3	1.9	-2	0	1.3	1	.5	.6	-2	.1414
3	9.3	.74	8.9	-3	2.9	-2	.6	1.3	-1	.5	0	9	.9999
4	9.3	.74	8.9	-3	1.9	2	1.3	1.3	-1	.8	.6	14	.9999
5	9.3	.74	8.9	3	.7	2	1	-1	1	.4	.5	17	.9999
6	9.3	.74	8.9	3	2.9	2	1.3	1.3	-1	0	.6	20	.9999
7	9.3	.74	8.9	-3	2.2	-2	1.5	1.3	-1	.2	.5	9.2	.9999
8	9.3	.74	8.9	3	1.9	-2	1.3	-1	1	.5	0	14	.9999
9	9.3	.74	-9	-3	1	2	1.3	1.3	1	.3	0	-4	.0134
10	9.3	.74	8.9	-3	2.3	2	.4	1.3	1	.2	.8	-3	.0392

Using training data to derive a classifier and then to estimate the accuracy of the classifier can result in misleading overoptimistic estimates due to overspecialization of the learning algorithm (or model) to the data. In the holdout method, the given data are randomly partitioned into two independent sets, a training set and a test set. Two thirds of the data are allocated to the training set, and the remaining one third is allocated to the test set. The training set is used to derive the classifier, whose accuracy is estimated with the test set (Han and Kamber, 2001). Random sub-sampling is a variation of the holdout method in which the holdout method is repeated three times in this study.

As a result of verification on the goodness-of-fit with the user data, seventy-three out of the total the a hundred and eight user samples were shown to be fit (table 83). The overall accuracy estimate is 67% in suggested model. This is taken as the average of the accuracies obtained from iteration.

The accuracy of index can be verified by how well they can predict the satisfaction. As the ground of index development is the interactivity-satisfaction model, the index that has the high correlation with the produced satisfaction index can be valid and really effective. Therefore, it is necessary to consider the correlation between the total indicators and the satisfaction index.

According to the index based on the interactivity-satisfaction model, it provides the significance on the viewpoint of user, system, input, and output. It turned out that the suggested index accounted the grip sense of input device. This shows that the grip sense for the use of input device is a significant expositive variable that users can acquire through their experience in the ubiquitous service environment. In the provision of ubiquitous service, the variable that users can control the most actively is the interface. Thus, the importance of the multimodal interface must be emphasized enough (u_{21}).

Though it may be different from the person-to-person service, the user also needs the user admission time to wait after the request of ubiquitous service. This shows the importance of the system performance. In the viewpoint of user, it means the storage capacity of the system (s_5). Thus, we can see that the time is an important consideration in the interactivity for ubiquitous service users. As for the web service, the time variables such as feedback time and spending time are emphasized here too.

For the design of ubiquitous service with excellent interactivity, we need the system that has two or more multimodal interfaces and the input device with the sensitive grip.

5. Interactivity index applications and tool support

5.1 Introduction of evaluation tool

An application system has been developed to use the suggested metric and conceptual model. The application system provides the definition of interactivity index, standards and metric. It also gives us the map of hierarchical relations between the interactivity evaluation indicators, and the plan and guide for the evaluation of interactivity. It supports us to choose and evaluate the diverse indicators for the interactivity evaluation in the ubiquitous service that may be defined too broadly to be used easily. According to the standard, the indicators and factors are chosen and the data for their quantification are collected. For example, if a developer wants to develop a revised interactive service, he or she can receive the evaluation plan and guide of interactivity from this tool. The former interactivity evaluation plan can be managed continuously with the revised plan in this system, and the change trace of evaluation methods and the trend analysis of interactivity are also possible (Pinelle and Gutwin, 2003).

For the application of suggested metric and model, an editor was developed. u-SIM editor provides an integrated tool box with which the un-experienced personnel can also perform the interactivity evaluation. The developed evaluation systems can be classified into the task-driven evaluation and the element driven (non-task) evaluation (Wang and Garlan, 2000; Russell et al., 2002). In case of task-driven evaluation, it performs according to the process of service scenario. Meanwhile, the element-driven evaluation tool performs the evaluation on the general interactivity factors regardless of the task. So, it evaluates the factors in a random order (figure 28).

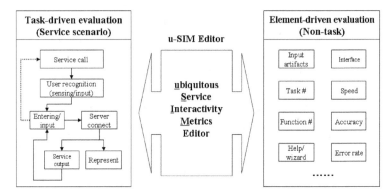

Figure 28. u-SIM editor component

We developed the u-SIM editor to support the kinds of activities just described and as a first step towards an integrative interactivity evaluation toolbox for practitioners who may not be experts in interactivity (or usability) engineering. The characteristics of u-SIM editor are as follows. First, u-SIM editor provides the diverse visual information on the relation of data with the service components, attributes, indicators, and metric. Second, u-SIM editor provides the repository to restore and compare the results of interactivity evaluation. Therefore, we can draw out and compare diverse combination of attributes, indicators and evaluations from it. Figure shows the screen shots of some systems.

It carries out the evaluation through the system with the evaluation order and components planed according to the characteristics of ubiquitous service (figure 29). The editor supports a multi-views visual exploration of the relations among sets of interaction unit, sub-component, and interactivity index. A repository of interactivity evaluation results for different combinations of indicators can be created and saved with the u-SIM editor. There are also a few wizards in the editor that are intended to help developers or testers who may not be already familiar with interactivity (or usability) engineering to create a concrete, step-by-step evaluation stage for a set of u-Services.

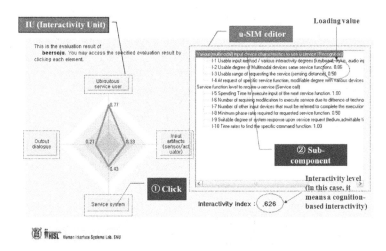

Figure 29. u-SIM editor output main interface

5.2 Application of evaluation tool

The automatic evaluation tool developed through the suggested metric and model are to perform the sequence shown in table 84.

Table 84. Interactivity evaluation process of u-Service

Sequence	Phase	Contents
1	Item selection	• Interactivity evaluation: selection of components, attributes, and indicators
2	Order selection	• Analysis on the provision stage of ubiquitous services • Determination of evaluation order of interactivity indications
3	Evaluation performance	• Performs the evaluation on the basis of selected evaluation indicators
4	Result analysis	• Determines the interactivity level • Diagnoses the general level including the experts opinions

The result of case study is essential for priority of design variables. u-SIM editor is focused on interactivity evaluation on u-Home service.

It was designed for the contents of ubiquitous service that was to be evaluated, classified into scenario and arranged in order to reflect them to the evaluation.

The developed tool will give much help to users and developers with its interactivity components, indicators and evaluation methods in the ubiquitous service when they are trying to improve the existing service or to develop a new service. Moreover, it provides the interpretation, definition and exposition of indicators: the diagnosis in the level of interactivity, the swift search performance, and the extensibility to add new model functions. If a new evaluation plan is established, it sets up the definition and range, and calculates the levels automatically with the collection of each indicator. It also enables to extend the standard evaluation method and the new interactivity indicators.

Part IV: Conclusion

6. Discussion and conclusion

6.1 Discussion

This study started from the still-subtle concept of ubiquitous service. While considering the design elements of ubiquitous service, this study has suggested the human-system interaction capability (interactivity) metric, which are the integrated metric derived from a large-scale experiment that was attempted for the evaluation of ubiquitous service. The metric is based on the evaluation technique of person-to-person service and the satisfaction quality (usability, ease-of-use, etc.). This study suggested fifty-one metric that are important in the design of ubiquitous service, and selected twenty-two metric for the interactivity of ubiquitous service.

We have discussed what scopes have to be considered in designing the user-centered ubiquitous services. It has classified the interactivity characteristics in terms of four different categories. The framework proposed is mainly based on the literature while some resulting from empirical survey in the industry. Therefore, we are carefully arguing that the evaluation scopes and the interactivity metrics may not be fully applicable in the current industry. Even through, this study is promising many implications to the current ubiquitous service. This chapter will investigate how equally the evaluation scopes we have proposed and the interactivity characteristics could be matched with the current technological feasibility of the ubiquitous services, so we can see what benefits and the deficiencies of the proposed framework would be.

The summary of the study results are as follows:

First, the development of interactivity evaluation metric and the large scale evaluation experiment. In this study, we have suggested the metric for the ubiquitous service that are experienced in real life, and introduced the concept of ubiquitous service interactivity, drawing out more than eighty factors and defining fifty-one metric.

Second, design variable selection and hierarchical model building using the quantification I-type analysis. To carry out the verification necessary for the normalization after the development of metric, we built up the interactivity-satisfaction model through the diverse factors that compose the interactivity of ubiquitous service. Moreover, in methodology, we used the quantification I-type analysis according to the psychometric theory to find the structure of evaluation indicators for the interactivity of ubiquitous service. We drew out twenty-two metric that compose the interactivity of ubiquitous service. The suggested models were turned out to be effective to estimate the interactivity and overall satisfaction on the ubiquitous service in common. The 'user experience', 'contextualization', 'ubiquity', and 'service capability' were shown to be the main component in this framework.

Third, the development of interactivity index. Though the derived indicators, we developed the interactivity evaluation index for the ubiquitous service. For the development, Logistic Regression (LR) was used, and the verification of the index was carried out its *odds* of classification using data set. In this study, we calculated the interactivity index of ubiquitous service from the suggested metric through the user scenario method. The result of the interactivity model implies that it will predict the satisfaction better when the ubiquitous service is measured in four classified dimensions. Therefore, the index development was aimed to draw out the sub-indicators of the ubiquitous service evaluation and the performance degree. Through the developed performance degrees, we evaluated the attributes of ubiquitous service to calculate the loading value for each one. The calculated loading value was compared with the first result. We confirmed the relation between the interactivity and the satisfaction, and very carefully concluded that we could accept the index that explained the interactivity by analyzing it into nine indicators.

Fourth, the prototype tool development of ubiquitous service interactivity metric. For the application of the suggested metric and conceptual model, we developed an application tool and editor. The tool developed to evaluate the characteristics of ubiquitous service components can provide the definition of the factors, indicators, and metrics. Moreover, it supplies the radio-chart on the structural relation among indicators. Finally, it shows the current level of ubiquitous service interactivity through the index.

The methods toward to find the interactivity metrics have two approaches: one is the questionnaire anchoring approach concerning user's recognition between the ubiquitous service interactivity and the measuring indicator; and the other is the approach whether to include user test results into the performance measure.

As a result of questionnaire anchoring, we found that the key attribute of the interactivity was the contextualization, and that the next were the user experience, service capabilities, and ubiquity in order. Users thought it is most important to provide the service that is appropriate to the context concerning the relation between the service and the user. Meanwhile, they evaluated the portability or connectivity of ubiquity a little lower. The mobility and the ubiquity are the attributes with high importance in the mobile services. So, they seemed to be evaluated a lower in the interactivity attributes of ubiquitous service. The difference from the person-to-person service was the importance of back-end performance. That is, in case of service capability support which cannot be found in the person-to-person service and is the specific attribute of ubiquitous service environment, the response between the user and the system becomes a very important indicator in improving its interactivity.

According to the calculation of loading value (degree of priority), we have suggested four components (user, input artifacts, service systems, output artifacts) and eight characteristics (perception, manipulation, recognition, service call, integration, capsulation, browsing/execution, personalization). The most important component was turned out to be the input artifacts (sensor, actuator); recognition, and the least important was the output artifacts (multimedia); personalization. The 'personalization' is the attribute to supply the appropriate service to the user automatically through their experience. As the

142

personalization was experienced through the only one experience rather than the learning effects, the system seemed not to be able to personalize the experience properly and provided the service to make an experimental error and limitation. In case of user-perception, the indicator concerning the expectation level and effort level of user turned out to be more important than the measuring indicator of effective-efficient recognition in the ubiquitous service response. In case of service capability; integration and capsulation, the integrity and agreeability between the service components and the information supplying capacity were shown as important. Smailagic et al. (2001) have evaluated the ubiquitous service, mainly focusing on the features, and the balance of attention between the device and the physical environment, and context-awareness service functionality. We listed several of our findings, suggesting in parentheses the appropriate evaluation scopes from our framework.

For the user experience support characteristics, we developed fourteen metric variables but drew out only seven significant metric through the experiment. Among them, the most important was 'the occasion number that the user loses the control during the service use'. In case of user experience support that supports the interactivity of ubiquitous service, the fewer (less than twice) the user loses the control of use and the lower the effort level of user becomes during the use of ubiquitous service, the higher the interactivity felt by the user becomes (user-perception; input artifacts-service call). There are variables that must be considered in the service design: the number of I/O supplied from the ubiquitous service must be reduced (task ratio<.2, i.e. the ratio to the tasks must be kept less than .2. If the tasks are 10, the devices must be less than 2); the quantity of information sent from the client to the server must be minimized; and the stand-by time for the performance of other input service function must also be reduced (stand-by time<30 sec, i.e. the time to serve the result and to find the next order must be less than 30 seconds).

In case of contextualization support characteristic, we developed fourteen metric variables but chose only four significant metric through the experiment. The occurred to be most important was 'the duration time for user to revise the procedure through the convenience and experience'. In case of user experience support which is the most important among the interactivity characteristics of ubiquitous service, the higher the intuitional recognition degree on the service response becomes and the less the error cases with the provision of intuitionally recognizable results become during the use of ubiquitous service, the higher the interactivity felt by the user becomes (user-perception; output artifacts-browsing/execution). As the variables to be considered in the design, minimizing the error task and/or the User Operating Time (UOT) was suggested (ratio<.2, i.e. the ratio of error to the total user's operation time must be designed to be less than .2).

In case of ubiquity support characteristic, we developed eleven metric variables but chose only six significant metric through the experiment. Among them, we found that 'the application degree of multimodal devices when specific service functions are demanded' was the most important. In case of user experience support which is the interactivity of ubiquitous service, the importance of the use of multimodal interface was emphasized (user-manipulation; input artifacts-recognition). As a variable to be considered in the design, the extensibility of interface was suggested. The number of interfaces used in the experiment was from 1.7 to 1.9, which is less than 2. As this number is similar to that of interfaces supplied by the mobile services, we can see that the development and/or extension of multimodal device and/or interface are very critical.

In case of service capability support characteristic, we developed twelve metric variables but chose only five significant metric through the experiment. Among them, we found that 'the temporary repository and/or buffering function' was the most important. In case of service capability support, it is the most distinctive attribute of ubiquitous service that is different from the person-to-person service. In the back-end side for the evaluation of interactivity, it works the role, for instance, the server of the person-to-person service. The lower 'the stability degree according to the addition and/or deletion of service function' or the change rate of response time according to the addition and/or deletion of service function is, the higher the interactivity felt by the user becomes (service system-integration, -capsulation; output artifacts-browsing/execution). The most important variable to be considered in the service design was the maintenance of response time rate during the extension of functions (positive effects; ratio<.2, i.e. it must be designed to keep less than 20% of existing service response time when a service is added). Also the number of help calls for the confirmation and interpretation on the service result must be minimized (mean number<3, i.e. the average callings must be less than 3).

Generally speaking, users of ubiquitous service showed a tendency of uncertainty avoidance. In case of u-Education, we could see the importance of co-works such as a remote meeting (parents-children) and convention (tele-works, mobile works). In case of Computer Supported Cooperative Work (CSCW), it seemed that the remote business support systems such as u-Work would be available in the future.

Meanwhile, we found that, as a negative side-effect, the interactivity of ubiquitous service could enhance the isolation of the user from the state-of-the-world. Therefore, it is important to develop the user-technology with non-technological elements that make human beings more human. The user of ubiquitous service can start the service through the service recognition, and use it through the ubiquitous attributes in the input devices. The service system can supply the most appropriate service to the user by recognizing the user's situation. Through the system capacity, the output artifacts become possible, and it finally returns to the user's experience to complete service process with the high quality of interactivity.

6.2 Conclusion and contribution of the study

The ubiquitous service is developing, like all ordinary merchandises, to meet diverse demands of users. The ubiquitous service is aiming to supply the convenience and benefit to people and finally to enhance the welfare of users. The evaluation of service experiences is very useful to develop the better service. However, at this point where the commercial use of ubiquitous service is about to start, its prototype and/or test-bed are too scarce. In general, for other services and products, we could select some expert users and let them evaluate the prototype goods to solve the problems early stage (user testing, usability test, etc.). However, in case of ubiquitous service system, computers have to be installed in every sites of environment and the service has to be supplied to users through the service systems. Moreover, we have to meet the diverse demands of users with different characters. Even though we put aside the problem whether the realization of technological function 'comprehending the human intention through many sensors and calculating to treat it like the human sense' could be possible, the evaluation on the ubiquitous service also becomes very complex and difficult. Although the personal difference of users may be small, it sometimes can work a critical role. Therefore, when considering all these factors, the evaluation of interactivity in the ubiquitous service is very difficult. In spite of these restrictions and insufficiencies, this study tried to develop the metric for the evaluation of interactivity for the ubiquitous service. We thought that suggesting an appropriate model for the interactivity could be sufficiently meaningful in the future development of ubiquitous service systems.

In all the environmental difficulties, we made efforts to suggest a tool to evaluate the interactivity of ubiquitous service. The interactivity was evaluated from the users who had the preconception that whatever service connected with 'u (ubiquitous)' could be the futuristic service. 'So was the functional evaluation concerning the design variables?'. When compared with existing services, the ubiquitous service has peculiar attributes. We developed the studies that could reflect the attributes and carried out the validation work for the standardization through the psychometric theory. To verify the suggested metric, we made a questionnaire experiment, and estimated the final influential variable from the result as well as the index. Through this process, we tried to develop the evaluation tool that can be used in the field by the designer and the developer.

To evaluate the interactivity-satisfaction of the ubiquitous service users, we suggested the interactivity quantitative metric by using the ubiquitous attributes. In the effects of ubiquitous service, we sought to include items that are hard for quantification, such as the pleasure and convenience of users, as well as the physically measurable items such as time and cost reduction. If we adopt the methodology with the utility function for each indicator in ubiquitous service, the satisfaction degree of users may be quantified through the interactivity evaluation.

The contributions of this study are as follows:

First, this study extended and/or suggested the interactivity evaluation method as an extension of utility evaluation method that is required in the development of product and service. The interactivity includes the utility aspect in the result of the service use, and the quality evaluation aspect in the inter-personal service aspect. As the evaluation of the personal service quality cannot be made definitely in the way of success and/or failure but is concerned with the satisfaction of user, effort and pride etc., the interactivity evaluation method was suggested to reflect the psychological dimension in the emotional quality evaluation. We also endeavored to extend the existing interactivity factor of function-based and cognition-based attributes into that of Measures of Perceived Interactivity (MPI) and activity-based attributes fit for the ubiquitous service.

Second, this study developed an evaluation methodology to evaluate the interactivity in the ubiquitous service. The model and the methodology suggested here are to analyze the current status and level of ubiquitous services. As shown in the related studies, there have been many attempts to develop the design guideline, metric, and evaluation techniques for the ubiquitous service computing, but there were no contents for the user's evaluation on the service. Most of the research methods concerning the ubiquitous environment are the same as conventional ones in the IT era. Therefore, they cannot fully reflect the characteristics of ubiquitous service. To select a space-time necessary for the realization of ubiquitous service among many space-times that users can come to confront and to serve a service appropriate to the characteristics of each space-time, we need the evaluation methodology that comprehends the importance of space-time and reflects its characteristics. The conventional user evaluation techniques cannot satisfy this condition. It is because the conventional techniques have focused on evaluating the quality of specific applications

147

(Abowd, 1998; Kim, 2000; Bing, 2001).

Third, this study defined the components and indicators to evaluate the interactivity of ubiquitous service as a role of person-to-person service. A conceptual framework is necessary to understand ubiquitous services. We suggested a framework of user's activity evaluation for the ubiquitous service to extend the understanding of digital user activity. Related studies on the ubiquitous service also used the profile information on users, but they had difficulty in systematic approaches such as ontological application and had little consideration on the services by other devices than user's hand-held ones. However, this study provided a guideline enabling the sustainable service development by suggesting four components and eight functions of ubiquitous service.

Fourth, this study suggested an evaluation method integrating the ubiquitous service and the attributes of product. The concepts of productized services (clear definition of service, standardization of services, common threads of service components, reusability and flexibility) and servicized products (add services values to exiting products, create values through entire product life cycle) reflect the service attribute evolving to the everyday service (Angel, 2004; Sako et al., 2006; Min, 2007). It also suggested an evaluation method integrating the ubiquitous service and the product. The suggested framework has the significance in that it provided a connecting chain among the ubiquitous environment, service, business, and user evaluation system for the first time. This guideline can be applied to the real business at once as well as to the academic study.

Fifth, we developed a tool that can evaluate the components of ubiquitous service with the attributes of ubiquitous service interactivity. We defined the interaction unit of scale with the evaluation unit of level, and suggested an integrated evaluation tool for the ubiquitous service (ubiquitous Service Interactivity Metrics: u-SIM). This tool is to provide the industry with insights into how to measure the ubiquitous services, to inform academia of how to prepare the business model for ubiquitous services.

Sixth, while carrying out the study on the research method for the evaluation of interactivity between the ubiquitous service and the user, we suggested the evaluation index to estimate the service level required by the ubiquitous service supplier or designer in the beginning. The evaluation index for the interactivity ubiquitous service enables to evaluate and/or compare the service comprehensibly and supports the decision-making. This study carried out the first project for the comprehensive indexing of ubiquitous service to determine and compare the service level objectively on the basis of indicators.

Seventh, this study adopted more developed analysis technology than conventional regressive formula. In the former analysis process of affective engineering, it was not sufficient to apply the model to deal with the diverse responses of user. In diverse view points, it applied the analysis methods to the simply ordered data without the hierarchy of response such as the ordered logit model. Especially, in applying the model to deal with the selection of ordered polytomous, we used the multiple logistic regression and General Linear Model (GLM) for the derivation of index, and the κ-mean clustering method for the adjustment of variances on the basis of psychometric theory to analyze the personal data with the subjective evaluation standards, and then checked the sensitivity of examinees who evaluated each design variable by grouping the appropriate level of design variables. Among them, we selected the design variables that are statistically meaningful and appropriate to the technological interpretation and then re-adjusted the level of design variables.

The result of this study can be applied as follows:

First, it can be used to analyze the potential users of the service by evaluating the interactivity level of ubiquitous service. Its application to the development of suggested framework service can be helpful in collecting the demands of potential service users and apprehending their levels. In the situation, the boundary between product and service is disappearing; we may extend the usability evaluation concept of 'everyday product' to the evaluation concept of interactivity.

Second, it can be used for the establishment of Ubiquitous service Strategy Planning (USP). As an upgrade of Information Strategy Planning (ISP), the USP is being applied for the strategy establishment in the new industrial fields. If the suggested methodology and framework are used, we can develop unique models to apply many services to specified environments. In the future, as the user-centered technologies are developed the systems to response actively to the human emotion and all the technologies are evolved to be convenient to us, we can construct the residence environment upgraded in ubiquity and welfare (Kim, 2007). As a strategy to adapt to the ubiquitous service society, it can be the evaluating indicator for the development of emotion transmitting technique, communication activating and emerging technique, and the service platform of human, environment, and technique convergence. In reality, it was applied to a company town that is being developed as a u-City, and reduced the service developing period for the city by two weeks. Through the application of methodology that can support the service platform development, it accomplished visible effects such as the reduction of developing period and costs.

Third, it can contribute to the extension of 'u-Readiness' policy. Before 2000, the information indicator was applied to diagnose the development stage of IT and the result was used as the data for establishing the strategy and execution plan (Jung, 2007). To measure the preparedness of ubiquitous society that becomes more intellectualized in all aspects of the nation, more complex indicators are required. The networked-readiness is developed for World Economic Forum (WEF), the convergence-readiness in England, and mobile-readiness in Finland to be used as a ubiquitous computing indicator. As the past models of information level diagnosis are confined to specific areas, they can hardly explain the advance to the ubiquitous society. So, the indicators concerning the social acceptance and readiness of ubiquitous technology (violation of private information and privacy, information gap, and security etc.) are considered important now (Toshio, 2005). The comprehensive indicators suggested in this study can provide a motive to develop the u-Readiness to measure the extension and application degrees of Ubiquitous Technology (UT) in the whole society that is being promoted in Korea as well.

We have suggested diverse contributions and applications of this study, but the result of this study has a limitation because of following reasons:

First, there was a difficulty in choosing the objects of experiment. As the ubiquitous services to be evaluated are being served very diversely now, and they are not widely experienced services, there is an experimental difficulty. In this study, we made an experiment on the u-Home service among the diverse ubiquitous services in a recently constructed experience hall. This selection was just one for the experimental convenience rather than the experimental approach to apply it to a specific industry domain. When considering the environmental characteristics of ubiquitous service, there must be some inherent limitation in actualization of the environment at a small laboratory. However, to construct the large-scale experimental environment, we have to pay too much cost (for the space, equipment, etc.). Thus, unlike the evaluation of other products or services, there is some limitation in choosing the objects for evaluation. Therefore, the interactivity indicators derived from this study should be examined once more in each industry (e.g.: u-Factory, etc.) after some years when the ubiquitous services become more common.

Second, there was a limitation in experimental method. In this study, we made a large-scale experiment in the small experimental environment, which was almost an impossible project. To overcome the temporal limitation and the environmental defects, we adopted an interactivity evaluation method based on the scenario-task. This scenario-task evaluation method may cause the different result from that of direct experience (Newman and Lamming, 1995; Jokela et al., 2006; Kristen et al., 2006). Even for the low level of ubiquitous services, if the user observation method (e.g.: ethnographic, anthropology) is applied through the direct experience of interactivity, it will fundamentally show more precise results.

Third, there was a limitation in the level of experimental objects. This study has a problem of containing the low level ubiquitous services. The essential difference of ubiquitous service from existing service is that the most appropriate service is supplied not by the request of users but by the recognition of service supplier (service system). To be a high-level ubiquitous service, it has to collect the whole information on the user, and calculate the characteristics of the user to serve the most appropriate service. In such case, the user and the service system must be connected without pause in the environment. Moreover, the service must be served in a quiet way rather than the complex or annoying way to the user when he and/or she want the service. But, this aspect could not be included in the scenario or item development. It was also difficult to have the examinees fully understand the essence of ubiquitous service. In viewpoint of measurement, it means that the object of evaluation becomes vague. In addition, as the ubiquitous service is made through the combination and extension of computing technology installed in the user's environment, the users even may not recognize such service in their environment. Therefore, the evaluation on the interactivity of high-level ubiquitous service may be hard to measure, and to devise a new evaluation methodology will be a future task of this study.

Fourth, the suggested index did not count the cost-justifying factors (return on investment, cost and effect, etc.). The suggested index for the interactivity of ubiquitous service was checked in their contention of user, but not in their economy. If the economic aspect were included into the first study, the study might become more complex or even erroneous. However, as an update of all technologies advance, the ubiquitous service requires the service system containing the highly expensive technologies. Introduction of this kind of service system will inevitably impose the economic burden to both of the supplier and the consumer. In addition to the cost for the validity examination of the project, if the efforts to enhance the interactivity of ubiquitous service raises the economic burden that cannot be taken by the user, this technology cannot be used in practice. Therefore, the addition of the evaluation indicator for the service evaluation on the price, brand value, etc. is necessary in the stage of planning.

Fifth, there is a limitation in the analysis method. In the HCI part of affective (Kansei) engineering, the analysis of significance according to the structure of indicators has mainly suggested to be done with Structural Equation Model (SEM) through Confirmatory Factor Analysis (CFA). In this study, however, we used quantification I-type analysis, General Linear Model (GLM) and Multiple Regression (MR) through Exploratory Factor Analysis (EFA). The indexing of evaluation indicators was developed with the final influential variable derived from the GLM and MR. Because of this: we studied the possibility of the multicollinearity phenomenon among the candidate variables happening. In case of the estimate y model y_1 to y_4 at the first stage of analysis, we established the model in consideration of the multicollinearity, but the final multicollinearity among the candidate variables composing the estimate y was ignored. As a result, in case of Logistic Regression (LR) belong used for the development of index, the index derived from the first fifty-one metrics and that from the selected twenty-two metric was fairly different in the probability and the precision. In the future study, the more probable index seems to be developed if we use all the candidate variables including the estimate y.

Future work focuses on testing and comparing the ubiquitous service interactivity of different tasks used for conversational emotional quality (e.g.: Calmness) evaluations. Furthermore, we plan the development a measurement methodology for 'perceived interactivity and/or activity-based interactivity'. Thus, we will be able to obtain a more comprehensive big picture about ubiquitous service users, their conversational activities and their perception of service delay.

People are trying to utilize the ubiquitous service in practice through the diverse conceptual approaches in the comprehensive viewpoint of product and service. Typical approaches are as follows: the first is the evolutionary approach that sees the ubiquitous service as the convergence paradigm (convergence and/or divergence) with symbiosis characteristics that provides the different attributes in total (IBM, 2007). As the ubiquitous service has a characteristic of complementarities as like productized services and/or servicized products, if one of the two complementary features is completely satisfied, the other side becomes unsatisfactory. Therefore, there is an approach to find the compromising point. The second is the attempt to define the development type of ubiquitous service through the contacting

153

level with the customers (high-contact, low-contact). On the marketing level of ubiquitous service (seven Ps: Product, Pricing, Place, Promotion, Participants, Process of service assembly, and Physical evidence), the high contact service used to be considered as the user-centered service, and the low contact service as equipment-centered service (Booms and Bitner, 1981; Lee, 1998; Loucopoulos, 2003). In case of ubiquitous service with the mixed customer contacts, the service participants (user and service agencies) that are a characteristic of high-contact service become the most important strategic elements. Because of this characteristic of the user-centered service, the service environment and the procedure become important elements, too. This kind of approach demands the continuous large scale researches on the interactivity evaluation of user-centered ubiquitous service.

Regardless of sill being in the incipient stage, the ubiquitous service technology has the sufficient potential to provide the innovative computer-based service systems such as the decision-making system that can offer us the personalized and prompt service. The concepts and results of ubiquitous service can promote the existing computer-based service system in some important areas. As it can be used to comprehend the situation information of users and to draw out the recommendation items from the situation information, the interactivity technology of ubiquitous service will be very adequate to the current intelligent service system. If the performance of a service system is raised by the interactivity technology of ubiquitous service, the more profit can be guaranteed through the higher efficiency and the business environment can be supported with the higher effectiveness.

Reference

Aarts, E., and Marzano, S. (2003), *The New Everyday: Views on Ambient Intelligence,* Uitgeverij 010 Publishers, Rotterdam, Netherlands.

Abowd, G. D. (1998), Software design issues for ubiquitous computing, *Proceedings of VLSI (Very Large Scale Integration) System Level Design,* IEEE Computer Society Workshop 1998, USA.

Abowd, G. D., and Mynatt, E. D. (2000), *Charting past, present, and future research in ubiquitous computing, Special issue on human-computer interaction in the new millennium, Part 1,* ACM Press, USA.

Agresti, A. (1996), *An Introduction to Categorical Data Analysis,* John Wiley & Sons, Inc., NY, USA.

Akıllı, G. K. (2005), User Satisfaction Evaluation of an Educational Website, *the Turkish Online Journal of Educational Technology (TOJET)* 4(1), Article 11.

Alahuhta, P., and Heinonen, S. (2003), *Ambient Intelligence in Everyday Life: Housing,* Research report VTT Technical Research Center of Finland 2223.

Angel, R. (2004), Sustaining profitable customer relationships requires real leadership, *Ivey Business Journal* 11/12.

Arnstein, L., Kang, J. H., and Borriello, G. (2006), *Evaluation Scope for Ubiquitous Computing,* Intel Research Lab., Seattle, USA.

Asubonteng, P., McCleary, K. J., and Swan, J. E. (1996), SERVQUAL revisited: a critical review of service quality, *Journal of Services Marketing* 10(6).

Babakus, E., and Boller, G. W. (2002), An empirical assessment of the SERVQUAL scale, *Journal of Business Research* 24(3): 253-268.

Barkhuus, L., and Dey, A. (2003), Is context-aware computing taking control away from the user three levels of interactivity examined, *Proceeding of the 5th International Conference on Ubiquitous Computing:* 149-156.

Barki, H., and Hartwick, J. (1994), Measuring User Participation, User Involvement, and User Attitude, *MIS Quarterly* 18(1): 59-82.

Barnard, P., May, J., Duke, D., and Duce, D. (2002), Macrotheory for Systems of Interactors, *in* John M. Carroll (eds.), *Human-Computer Interaction in the New Millennium,* Addison-Wesley, ACM Press, NY.

Barton, J. J., and Kindberg, T. (2001), The cooltown user experience, *Proceedings of CHI2001,* Seattle, USA.

Bartram, L., and Czerwinski, M. (2002), Design and evaluation of notification interfaces for ubiquitous computing, *UbiComp02 Workshop 9.*

Basu, P., Ke, W., and Little, T. D. C. (2001), Metrics for Performance Evaluation of Distributed Application Execution in Ubiquitous Computing Environments, *Proceeding ACM UbiComp01 Workshop on Evaluation Methodologies for Ubiquitous Computing,* Atlanta, USA.

Bellotti, V., and Sellen, A. (1993), Design for privacy in ubiquitous computing environments, *Proceeding European Conference on Computer Supported Cooperative Work:* 77-92.

Bellotti, V., Back, M., Edwards, W. K., Grinter, R. E., Henderson, A., and Lopes, C. (2002), Making sense of sensing systems: Five questions for designers and researchers, *Proceedings of Conference Human Factors in Computing Systems*: 415-422.

BenMoussa, C. (2004), Supporting Salespersons through Location Based Mobile Applications and Services, *Proceedings of 4th International Conference on E-Commerce, E-Business, E-Government (I3E)*: 149-167.

Bertoa, M. F., Troya, J. M., and Vallecillo, A. (2006), Measuring the usability of software components, *The Journal of Systems and Software* 79: 427-439.

Beyer, H., and Holtzblatt, K. (1997), *Contextual Design: Defining Customer-Centered System,* Morgan Kaufmann.

Bing, J. W. (2001), Developing a Consulting Tool to Measure Process Change on Global Teams: The Global Team Process Questionnaire™, *Proceedings of Academy of Human Resource Development Conference 2001*, UK.

Blaine, A. P., Karim, A., and Bashar, N. (2005), Keeping ubiquitous computing to yourself: A practical model for user control of privacy, *International Journal of Human-Computer Studies* 63: 228-253.

Bonnie, E. J. (1996), Evaluation usability evaluation techniques, *ACM Workshop on strategic directions in computing research,* Carnegie Mellon University, Internal report.

Booms, B. M., and Bitner, M. J. (1981), Marketing strategies and organizational structure for service firms, *Marketing of Service*.

Borriello, G., Friedman, B., and Kahn, H. (2001), Ubiquitous computing: Technical, Psychological, and Value-Sensitive Integrations, *CHI 2001 Workshop on Distributed and*

157

Disappearing User Interfaces in Ubiquitous Computing, Seattle, USA.

Brinkman, W. P., Haakma, R., and Bouwhuis, D. G. (2007), Towards an empirical method of efficiency testing of system parts: A methodological study, *Interacting with Computers* 19: 342-356.

Brody, A., and Gottsman, E. (1999), Pocket BargainFinder: A handheld device for augmented commerce, *Proceedings of the international symposium on handheld and ubiquitous computing.*

Brooke, J. (1996), SUS: A "quick and dirty" usability scale, *in* Jordan, P. W., Thomas, B., Weerdmeester, A., and McClelland, A. (eds.), *Usability Evaluation in Industry,* London, Taylor and Francis: 189-194.

Bruseberg, A., and Philip, D. M. (2001), New product development by eliciting user experience and aspirations, *International Journal of Human Computer Studies* 55(4): 435-452.

Buckler, F., and Buxel, H. (2000), *Mobile Commerce Report,* http://www.profitstation.de/metafacts/press/M-commerce.htm.

Burgoon, J. K., Bonito, J. A., Bengtsson, B., Ramirez, Jr. A., Dunbar, N. E., and Miczo, N. (2000), Testing the interactivity model: Communication process partners assessments and the quality of collaborative work, *Journal of Management Information Systems* 16: 33-56.

Burnett, M., and Rainsford, C. P. (2001), A hybrid evaluation approach for ubiquitous computing environments, *Workshop on Evaluation Methodologies for Ubiquitous Computing 2001,* Atlanta, USA.

Burrell, J., Gay, G. K., Kubo, K., and Farina, N. (2002), Context-Aware Computing: A Test

Case, *Proceedings 4ᵗʰ International Conference Ubiquitous Computing:* 1-15.

Byun, J. Y. (2005), *A study on the human interface design application under the ubiquitous environment,* M.S. Thesis, Sookmyung Women's University, Korea.

Cagan, J., and Vogel, C. M. (2002), *Creating breakthrough products: Innovation from product planning to program approval,* Prentice-Hall Inc., NJ, USA.

Carolis, B., Pizzutilo, S., Palmisano, I., and Cavalluzzi, A. (2004), A personal agent supporting ubiquitous interaction, *Workshop from Objects to Agents:* 55-61.

Carr, C. L. (2002), A Psychometric Evaluation of the Expectations, Perceptions, and Difference-Scores Generated by the Is-Adapted SERVQUAL Instrument, *Decision Sciences* 33(2): 281-296.

Chin, J. P., Diehl, V. A., and Norman, K. (1998), Development of an instrument measuring user satisfaction of the human-computer interface, *In conference on Human Factors in Computing Systems, Association for Computing Machinery:* 213-218.

Cho, C. H., and Leckenby, J. D. (1997), *Internet-Related Programming Technology and Advertising,* Working Paper, Department of advertising, College of Communication, The University of Texas at Austin.

Cho, C. H., and Leckenby, J. D. (1999), Interactivity as Measure of Advertising Effectiveness: Antecedents and Consequences of Interactivity in Web Advertising, *Proceedings of Conference of the American Academy of Advertising:* 162-179.

Christensen, G. L., and Olson, J. C. (2002), Mapping consumers' mental models with ZMET, *Psychology & Marketing* 19(6): 477-502.

159

Chun, H. M., and Pyun, J. S. (2004), The Impact of Ubiquitous factors on Buyers' Purchase Intentions, *Proceedings of the Korea Society of Management Information Systems(KMIS) 2004:* 605-612.

Chung, D. B. (2005), *A study on the evaluation framework development for business model commercialization strategy in ubiquitous environment,* M.S. Thesis, Yonsei University, Korea.

Cohen, P. R., Johnston, M., McGee, D., Oviatt, S. L., Clow, J., and Smith, I. (1998), *The efficiency of Multimodal Interaction: A case study,* CHCC (Center for Human-Computer Communication) internal report, Oregon Graduate Institute of Science and Technology.

Constantine, L. L., and Lockwood, L. A. D. (1999), *Software for Use: A Practical Guide to the Models and Methods of Usage-Centered Design,* Addison-Wesley, NY, USA.

Cronin, J. J., and Taylor, S. A. (1992), Measuring service quality: A reexamination and extension, *Journal of Marketing* 56(3): 55-68.

Cronin, J. J., and Taylor, S. A. (1994), SERVPERF versus SERVQUAL: Reconciling performance-based and perceptions-minus-expectations measurements of service quality, *Journal of Marketing* 58(1): 125-131.

CUCN (National Center of Excellence for Ubiquitous Computing and Networking) (2005), Ubiquitous Computing System technology, *Center for Advanced RFID/USN Technology (CARUT) workshop,* Korea.

Da Costa, O., and Punie, Y. (2003), Ambient Intelligence in everyday life: A function-oriented science & technology roadmapping project, *Proceedings of New media, Technology and Everyday life in Europe Conference,* London.

160

Dag, J. N., Regnell, B., Madsen, O. S., and Aurum, A. (2001), An Industrial Case Study of Usability Evaluation in Market-Driven Packaged Software Development, *Proceedings of 9th international conference on Human-Computer Interaction,* New Orleans, USA.

Davies, N., and Gellersen, H. W. (2002), Beyond prototypes: Challenges in deploying ubiquitous systems, *Pervasive Computing* 1: 26-35.

Delen, D., Walker, G., and Kadam, A. (2004), Predicting breast cancer survivability: a comparison of three data mining methods, *Artificial Intelligence in Medicine* 34: 113-127.

Dey, A. K. (2001), Understanding and using context, *Personal and ubiquitous computing* 5(1): 4-7.

Dholakia, R. P., Zhao, M., Dholakia, N., and Fortin, D. R. (2000), Interactivity and revisits to websites: A theoretical framework, *Research Institute for Telecommunications and Information Marketing (RITIM) working paper.*

Diggle, P. J., Heagerty, P., Liang, K. Y., and Zeger, S. L. (2002), *Analysis of Longitudinal Data,* Oxford University Press, NY, USA.

Donnelly, M., and Shiu, E. (1999), Assessing service quality and its link with value for money in a UK local authority's housing repairs service using the SERVQUAL approach, *Total Quality Management* 10(4): 498-506.

Downes, E. J., and McMillan, S. J. (2000), Defining interactivity: A qualitative identification of key dimensions, *New Media & Society* 2(2): 157-179.

Dyke, T. P., Kappelman, L. A., and Prybutok, V. R. (1997), Measuring Information Systems Service Quality: Concerns on the use of the SERVQAUL Questionnaire, *MIS Quarterly* 21(2): 195-208.

Earthy, J. (1998-a), *Usability Maturity Model: Human-centered scale,* Technical report, INUSE Project.

Earthy, J. (1998-b), *Usability Maturity Model: Processes,* Technical report, INUSE Project.

Edenborough, R. (1998), *Using Psychometrics: A Practical Guide to Testing and Assessment,* Kogan Page.

Edwards, W. K., and Grinter, R. E. (2001), At home with ubiquitous computing: seven challenges, *Proceedings of UbiComp 2001:* 256-272.

Edwards, W. K., Bellotti, V., Dey, A. K., and Newman, M. W. (2003), The challenges of user-centered design and evaluation for infrastructure, *Proceedings of the SIGCHI conference on Human factors in computing systems.*

Ehn, P. (1988), *Work-oriented design of computer artifacts,* Falköping: Arbetslivscentrum/Almqvist & Wiksell International, Hillsdale, Lawrence Erlbaum Associates, NJ, USA.

Eleni, C., and Achilles, K. (2005), GAS Ontology: An ontology for collaboration among ubiquitous computing devices, *International Journal of Human-Computer Studies* 62: 664-685.

Evans, C., and Gibbons, N. J. (2006), The interactivity effect in multimedia learning, *Computers & Education* 46.

Fleisch, E., and Tellkamp, C. (2003), The challenge of identifying value creating ubiquitous computing applications, *Workshop on Ubiquitous Commerce, UbiComp03.*

Franze, G., Carotenuto, L., and Balestrino, A. (2006), New inclusion criterion for the stability of interval matrices, *Control Theory and Applications* 153: 478-482.

Friedewald, M., Costa, O. D., Punie, Y., Alahuhta, P., and Heinonen, S. (2005), Perspectives of ambient intelligence in the home environment, *Telematics and Informatics* 22: 221-238.

Garlan, D., Siewiorek, D., Smailagic, A., and Steenkiste, P. (2002), Project Aura: Toward distraction-free pervasive computing, *IEEE Pervasive Computing:* 22-31.

Gay, G., and Hembrooke, H. (2004), *Activity-Centered Design: An Ecological Approach to Designing Smart Tools and Usable Systems,* The MIT Press.

Gopalakrishnan, P. S. (2001), User Interface issues in Pervasive Computing, *NIST (National Institute of Standards and Technology) Pervasive Computing 2001 Conference.*

Greenacre, M. J. (1984), *Theory and application of correspondence analysis,* Academy press Inc., London.

Greenfield, A. (2006), *Everyware: The dawning age of ubiquitous computing, New Riders,* Berkeley, CA, USA.

Guion, L. A. (2006), *Conducting an In-depth Interview,* Institute of Food and Agricultural Sciences (IFAS), University of Florida.

H-Life (2007), *Future Home Showcase 'H-Life',* Hillstate Gallery, Seoul, Korea.

Ha, L., and James, E. L. (1998), Interactivity reexamined: A baseline analysis of early business web sites, *Journal of Broadcasting & Electronic Media* 42(4).

Hair, J. F., Rolph, E. A., Ronald, L. T., and William, C. B. (1998), *Multivariate Data*

Analysis, 5th edition, Prentice Hall.

Ham, J. J. (2006), *A study on deriving killer application and developing evaluation model of ubiquitous computing,* M.S. Thesis, Yonsei University, Korea.

Hammer, F., and Reichl, P. (2005), How to Measure Interactivity in Telecommunications, *44th FITCE (the Federation of Telecommunications Engineers of the European Community) Congress 2005,* Vienna, Austria.

Han J., and Kamber, M. (2001), *Data mining: Concepts and Techniques*, Morgan Kaufmann.

Hassanein, K., and Head, M. (2003), Ubiquitous Usability: Exploring Mobile Interfaces within the Context of a Theoretical Model, *Proceedings of the 15th Conference On Advanced Information Systems Engineering (CAiSE 2003),* Velden, Austria.

Heckmann, D. (2005), *Ubiquitous User Modeling,* Ph.D Dissertation, Universität des Saarlandes, Deuch.

Heeter, C. (1989), Implications of new interactive technologies for conceptualizing communication, *in* Salvaggio, J. L. and Bryant, J. (eds.), *Media use in the information age: Emerging patterns of adoption and consumer use,* Lawrence Erlbaum Associates: 217-235, NJ, USA.

Heeter, C. (2000), Interactivity in the context of designed experiences, *Journal of Interactive Advertising* 1(1).

Heikkinen, K. (2005), *Conceptualization of user-centric personalization management,* Ph.D Dissertation, Lappeenranta University of Technology, Finland.

164

Heikkinen, K., and Porras, J. (2005), Conceptualization of user-centric personalization management in ubiquitous Service provisioning, *in* EURESCOM (eds.), *Ubiquitous Services and Applications,* VDE VERLAG, Denmark.

Hoffman, D. L., and George, R. F. (1986), Correspondence Analysis: Graphical Representation of Categorical Data in Marketing Research, *Journal of Marketing Research* 23: 213-227.

Hoffman, D. L., and Novak, T. P (1996), Marketing in Hypermedia Computer-Mediated Environments: Conceptual Foundations, *Journal of Marketing* 60: 50-68.

Hollemans, C. (1999), User satisfaction measurement methodologies: Extending the user satisfaction questionnaire, *In Proceedings of HCI International '99 of the 8th International Conference on Human-Computer Interaction:* 1008-1012.

Holtjona, G., and Fiona, F. (2004), u-Commerce: Emerging trends and research issues, *Industrial Management and Data Systems* 104(9): 744-755.

Horvitz, E., Kadie, C., Paek, T., and Hovel, D. (2003), Models of Attention in Computing and Communication: From Principles To Applications, *Communications of the ACM* 46(3): 52-59.

Hull, R., Reid, J., and Kidd, A. (2002), *Experience Design in Ubiquitous Computing,* Client and Media Systems Laboratory, HP Technical Report: HPL-2002-115.

Hur, M. H. (1998), *Quantification Method I, II, III, IV,* Freedom academy, Korea.

IBM (2007), *Ubiquitous technology*, IBM Ubiquitous Computing Lab. (UCL) and Watson Lab.

Igbaria, M., Zinatelli, N., Cragg, P., and Cavaye, A. (1997), Personal computing acceptance factors in small firms: a structural equation model, *MIS Quarterly* 21(3): 279-305.

Intille, S. S. (2002), Designing a home of the future, *IEEE Pervasive Computing* 1: 80-86.

Iqbal, R., Sturm, J., Kulyk, O., Wang, J., and Terken, J. (2005), User-Centered Design and Evaluation of Ubiquitous Services, *23rd Annual International Conference on Design of Communication (SIGDOC 2005),* 138-145.

ISO 9126-1 (2001), *Software Engineering: product quality – Part 1: Quality model,* International Standards Organization, Geneva, Switzerland.

ISO 9126-2 (2001), *Software Engineering: product quality – Part 2: External metrics,* International Standards Organization, Geneva, Switzerland.

ISO 9126-3 (2001), *Software Engineering: product quality – Part 3: Internal metrics,* International Standards Organization, Geneva, Switzerland.

ISO 9126-4 (2001), *Software Engineering: product quality – Part 4: Quality in use metrics,* International Standards Organization, Geneva, Switzerland.

ISO 9241-9 (1998), *Ergonomic requirements for office work with visual display terminals (VDTs) – Part 9: Requirements for non-keyboard input devices,* International Standards Organization, Geneva, Switzerland.

ISO 9241-11 (1998), *Ergonomic requirements for office work with visual display terminals (VDTs) – Part 11: Guidance on usability,* International Standards Organization, Geneva, Switzerland.

ISO TR 18529 (2000), *Ergonomics (Ergonomics of human-system interaction) - Human-*

centred lifecycle process descriptions, International Standards Organization, Geneva, Switzerland.

ISO 20282 (2006), *Ease of operation of everyday products,* International Standards Organization, Geneva, Switzerland.

ISO/IEC 15939 (2002), *Software Engineering – Software Measurement Process,* International Standards Organization, Geneva, Switzerland.

ISO/IEC 25000 (2005), *Software Engineering – Software Product Quality Requirements and Evaluation (SQuaRE) - Guide to SQuaRE,* International Standards Organization, Geneva, Switzerland.

Jameson, A. (2003), Adaptive Interfaces and Agents, *in* Julie A. Jacko and Andrew Sears (eds.), *The Human-Computer Interaction Handbook,* Lawrence Erlbaum Associates, NJ.

Jenna, B., and Geri, K. G. (2002), E-graffiti: evaluating real-world use of a context-aware system, *Interacting with Computers* 14: 301-312.

Jiang, J. J., Klein, G., and Carr, C. L. (2002), Measuring Information System Service Quality: Servqual from the Other Side, *MIS Quarterly* 26(2): 145-166.

Jo, I. H. (2004), *SAS Lecture and Statistic consulting*, Youngjin.com press, Korea.

Jo, W. D., Lee, K. J., Lee, H. K., Kwon, O. B., Kim, K. G., and Lee, E. J. (2006), *Ubiquitous Paradigm and u-Society,* Jinhan M&B Inc., Korea.

John, S., Ippokratis, P., Kostas, S., Lazaros, P., and James, L. C. (2007), Agent based middleware infrastructure for autonomous context-aware ubiquitous computing services, *Computer Communications* 30: 577-591.

Johnson, R. A., and Wichern, D. W. (1988), *Applied Multivariate Statistical Analysis*, Second Edition, Prentice-Hall, London.

Jokela, T. (2001), *Assessment of user-centered design processes as a basis for improvement action*, Ph.D. Dissertation, University of Oulu, Finland.

Jokela, T., Koivumaa, J., Pirkola, J., Salminen, P., and Kantola, N. (2006), Methods for quantitative usability requirements: a case study on the development of the user interface of a mobile phone, *Personal and Ubiquitous Computing* 10: 345-355.

Jung, B. J. (2007), *Ubiquitous Society Measurement using IT Readiness*, Ubiquitous society study series 27, NIA(National Information society Agency).

Junglas, I. A., and Watson, R. T. (2003), u-Commerce: An experimental investigation of ubiquity and uniqueness, *Proceedings of 24th International Conference on Information Systems (ICIS):* 414-426.

Kakihara, M., and Sorensen, C. (2002), Mobility: An Extended Perspective, *Proceedings of 24th Hawaii International Conference on System Sciences (HICSS):* 1-14.

Kalakota, R., and Robinson, M. (2002), *The Mobile Economy*, McGraw-Hill, NY.

Kannan, P., Chang, A., and Whinston, A. (2001), Wireless Commerce: Marketing issues and possibilities, *Proceedings of 34th Hawaii International Conference on System Sciences(HICSS):* 9015-9021.

Kettinger, W. J., and Lee, C. C. (2005), Zones of tolerance: Alternative scales for measuring information systems service quality, *MIS Quarterly* 29(4): 607-621.

Kim, C. R. (2003), *MDS & Conjoint analysis using SAS*, Freedom Academy, Korea.

Kim, C. R. (2004), *SAS Statistical analysis*, Data Research & Communications (DR&C), Korea.

Kim, J. B. (2005), *Emotional information awareness in ubiquitous,* Ph.D Dissertation, Kangwon National University, Korea.

Kim, J. V. (2000), HCI in the Global Knowledge-based Economy; Designing to Support Worker Adaptation, *ACM Transactions on Computer-Human Interaction* 7(2).

Kim, S. A. (2007), *u-Society Concept Application Strategies,* Future Housing Forum 2007, Korea Housing Associates.

Kim, S. H. (2006), *Developing the instrument for evaluating the usability of ubiquitous services,* M.S. Thesis, Seoul National University, Korea.

Kim, S. H., Park, C. H., and Kim, C. T. (2006), The analysis of u-service experienceability for ubiquitous service evaluation, *The Korean Association for Survey Research* 7(1): 1-28.

Kiousis, S. (2002), Interactivity: a concept explication, *New Media & Society* 4: 355-383.

Kirakowski, J., and Corett, M. (1993), SUMI: the Software Usability Measurement Inventory, *British Journal of Educational Technology* 24: 210-212.

Kleef, E., Trijp, H. C. M., and Luning, P. (2005), Consumer research in the early stages of new product development: a critical review of methods and techniques, *Food Quality and Preference* 16(3): 181-201.

Kristen, K. G., Michael, D. B., and Sarah, P. E. (2006), A comparison of Usability between Voting Methods, *Proceedings of USENIX/Accurate EVT (Electronic Voting Technology) workshop,* Vancouver, Canada.

Kurt, I., Ture, M., and Kurum, A. T. (2007), Comparing performances of logistic regression, classification and regression tree, and neural networks for predicting coronary artery disease, *Expert Systems with applications* 34: 366-374.

Kwon, O. B., and Kim, J. H. (2005), Ubi-SERVQUAL: An Amended SERVQUAL Model for Assessing the Quality of Ubiquitous Computing Services, *Conference of the Korea Society of Management Information Systems,* Seoul, Korea.

Kwon, O., Yoo, K., and Suh, E., (2006), ubiES: Applying ubiquitous computing technologies to an expert system for context-aware proactive services, *Electronic Commerce Research and Applications* 5: 209-219.

Landrum, H., and Prybutok, V. (2004), A service quality and success model for the information service industry, *European Journal of Operational Research* 156(3): 628-642.

Langheinrich, M. (2002), A privacy awareness system for ubiquitous computing environments, *In Proceedings of UbiComp02.*

Lattin, J., Carroll, J. D., and Green, P. E. (2003), *Analyzing Multivariate Data,* Brooks/Cole-Thomson Learning, Inc., Canada.

Lee, E. J. (2006), Development of Human-Centered Service Selection Rules, *in* Jo, W. D. (eds.), *Ubiquitous Paradigm and u-Society,* Jinhan M&B Inc., Korea.

Lee, S. H. (2006), *The effects of ubiquitous attributes of mobile contents on perceived interactivity and behavioral outcome,* Ph.D. Dissertation, Seoul National University, Korea.

Lee, S. Y. (1998), *Product and Service Manufacturing Management*, Bobmunsa, Korea.

Lee, T. M. (2003), *The effects of components of interactivity on purchase intentions in mobile environments,* Ph.D. Dissertation, Seoul National University, Korea.

Lee, W. J. (2005), *The Effects of Ubiquitous interactivity characteristic of new product on adoption and diffusion,* Ph.D. Dissertation, Seoul National University, Korea.

Leonard, M., Jessup, and Robey, D. (2002), The relevance of social issues in ubiquitous computing environments, *Communications of the ACM* 45(12).

Lewis, J. R. (1995), IBM computer usability satisfaction questionnaires: Psychometric evaluation and instructions for use, *International Journal of Human-Computer Interaction* 7: 57-78.

Lewis, J. R. (1999), Tradeoffs in the design of the IBM computer usability satisfaction questionnaires. *In Proceedings of HCI International '99 of the 8th International Conference on Human-computer Interaction:* 1023-1027.

Lewis, J. R. (2002), Psychometric evaluation of the PSSUQ using data from five years of usability studies, *International Journal of Human-Computer Interaction* 14(3): 463-488.

Lin, H. X., Choong, Y., and Salvendy, G. (1997), A proposed index of usability: A method for comparing the relative usability of different software systems, *Behavior and Information Technology* 16: 267-277.

Lindenberg, J., Pasman, W., Kranenborg, K., Stegeman, J., and Neerincx, M. A. (2007), Improving service matching and selection in ubiquitous computing environments: a user study, *Personal and Ubiquitous Computing* 11: 59-68.

Loiacono, E. T., Watson, R. T., and Goodhue, D. L. (2000), WebQual: A website quality instrument, *Working paper 2000-126-0, University of Georgia.*

Lombard, M., and Snyder-Dutch, J. (2001), Interactive Advertising and Presence: A Framework, *Journal of Interactive Advertising* 1(2).

Loucopoulos, P. (2003), The S^3 (Strategy-Service-Support) Framework for Business Process Modeling, *International workshop on Requirements Engineering for Business Process Support (REBPS'03),* Klagenfurt/Velden, Austria.

Lyytinen, K., and Yoo, Y. (2002), Issues and challenges in Ubiquitous Computing, *Communications of the ACM* 45(12): 63-65.

Mack, G. A., Lonergan, K., Scholtz, J., Steves, M. P., and Hale, C. R. (2004), A framework for metrics in large complex systems, *IEEE Aerospace conference proceedings* 5: 3217 - 3228.

Mallon, B., and Webb, B. (2000), Structure, causality, visibility and interaction: propositions for evaluating engagement in narrative multimedia, *International Journal of Human-Computer Studies* 53: 269-287.

Mankoff, J., and Carter, S. (2005), Crossing Qualitative and Quantitative Evaluation in the domain of Ubiquitous Computing, *CHI2005 Workshop 6,* Portland, USA.

Mankoff, J., Dey, A. K., Hsieh, G., Kientz, J., Ames, M., and Lederer, S. (2003), Heuristic evaluation of ambient displays, *Proceedings of the ACM CHI03 Conference on Human Factors in Computing Systems,* CHI Letters, 5(1).

Mardia, K. V., Kent, J. T., and Bibby, J. M. (1979), *Multivariate Analysis,* Academic Press, London.

Markett, C., Arnedillo, I., Weber, S., and Tangney, B. (2006), Using short message service to encourage interactivity in the classroom, *Computers & Education* 46(3): 280-293.

Maxwell, K. (2001), The Maturation of HCI Moving beyond Usability toward Holistic Interaction, *in* John M. Carroll (eds.), *Human-Computer Interaction in the New Millennium,* Addison-Wesley, ACM Press, NY.

McMillan, S. J. (1999), Four models of cyber-interactivity: Individual perceptions of interactivity in computer-mediated environments, *International Communication Association Annual Conference,* SF, CA.

McMillan, S. J. (2000), Interactivity is in the eye of the beholder: Function, perception, involvement, and attitude toward the web site, *Proceedings of the Conference of the American Academy of Advertising:* 71-78.

McMillan, S. J., and Hwang, J. S. (2002), Measures of Perceived Interactivity: An Exploration of the Role of Direction of Communication, User Control, and Time in Shaping Perceptions of Interactivity, *Journal of Advertising* 16(3).

Min, J. H. (2007), Concept, Trend, and Issues of Services Science, *Proceedings of The Korean Operations and Management Science Society:* Special session (Spring).

Moisen, G. G., and Frescino, T. S. (2002), Comparing five modeling techniques for predicting forests characteristics, *Ecological Modeling* 157: 209-225.

Mojsilovic, A., Ray, B., Lawrence, R., and Takriti, S. (2007), A logistic regression framework for information technology outsourcing lifecycle management, *Computers & Operations Research* 34: 3609-3627.

Morikawa, H., and Aoyama, T. (2004), Realizing the ubiquitous network: the internet and beyond, *Telecommunication Systems* 25: 449-468.

Muirhead, B. (2001), Interactivity Research Studies, *Educational Technology & Society* 4(3).

Muller, V. F. (1999), *Mobile Commerce Report,* Durlacher Research Ltd., London.

Myers, B., Hudson, S. E., and Pauch, R. (2000), Past, Present, and Future of User Interface Software Tools, *ACM Transactions on Computer-Human Interaction* 7(1).

Nakagawa, T., Yoshikawa, T., Ohta, K., Inamura, H., and Kurakake, S. (2004), Design and evaluation of scalable ubiquitous discovery system, *4th International Workshop on Application and Services in Wireless Networks (ASWN).*

Newhagen, J. E. (1998), Hitting the agenda reset button for the Internet: The problem of matching research with development, *International Communication Association Conference,* Jerusalem, Israel.

Newman, W. M., and Lamming, M. G. (1995), *Interactive System Design,* Addison-Wesley, Wokingham.

Nielsen, J. (1993), *Usability Engineering,* Morgan Kaufmann, SF, CA.

Nielsen, J. (1994), Heuristic evaluation, *in* J. Nielsen and R. L. Mack (eds.), *Usability Inspection Methods,* John Wiley & Sons, NY.

Nitecki, D. A. (1995), *An assessment of the applicability of SERVQUAL dimensions as customer-based criteria for evaluating quality of services in an academic library,* Ph.D. Dissertation, University of Maryland, USA.

Norman, D. A. (1999), *Invisible Computing; Why Good Products Can Fail, the Personal Computer Is So Complex and Information Appliances Are the Solution,* MIT Press.

Novak, T. P., Hoffman, D. L., and Yung, Y. F. (2000), Measuring the customer experience in online environments: a structural modeling approach, *Marketing Science* 19(1): 22-42.

Nunnally, J. C., and Bernstein, I. H. (1994), *Psychometric theory,* McGraw-Hill Inc.

Olson, G. M., and Olson, J. S. (2000), *Distance Matters,* Human-Computer Interaction 15(2): 139-178.

Parasuraman, A., and Zeithaml, V. A. (1994), Alternative scales for measuring service quality: A comparative assessment based on psychometric, *Journal of Retailing* 70(3): 201-230.

Parasuraman, A., Berry, L. L., and Zeithmal, V. A. (1988), SERVQUAL: A multiple-item scale for measuring customer perceptions of service quality, *Journal of Retailing* 64(1): 12-40.

Park, K. B. (2006), *Generalized Linear Model*, Hakjisa, Korea.

Peter, T., Christopher, S. C., Tian, X., and Myra, D. (2003), Evaluation of Visual Notification Cues for Ubiquitous Computing, UbiComp03, *Lecture Notes in Computer Science (LNCS)* 2864: 349-366.

Pinelle, D., and Gutwin, C. (2003), Task analysis for groupware usability evaluation: Modeling shared-workspace tasks with the mechanics of collaboration, *ACM transactions on Computer-Human Interaction* 10(4): 281-311.

Pitt, L. F., Opoku, R., and Hultman, M. (2007), What I say about myself: Communication of brand personality by African countries, *Tourism Management* 28: 835-844.

Preece, J., and Maloney, K. D. (2003), Online communities; Focusing on Sociability and usability, *in* Julie A. Jacko and Andrew Sears (eds.), *The Human-Computer Interaction Handbook,* Lawrence Erlbaum Associates, NJ.

Preece, J., Rogers, Y., and Sharp, H. (2002), *Interaction Design: beyond Human-Computer Interaction,* John Wiley & Sons, Inc., USA.

Pyun, J. M. (2005), *The optimization of the graphic user interface usability evaluation for mobile phone,* Ph.D. Dissertation, Dankook University, Korea.

QUIS (2003), *Questionnaire for user interaction satisfaction,* Online, available HTTP: http://www.lap.umd.edu/QUIS/index.html.

Rafaeli, S. (1998), Interactivity: From new media to communication, *in* R. P. Hawkins, J. M. Wieman and S. Pingree (eds.), *Advancing Communication Science: Merging Mass and Interpersonal Processes,* Newbury Park, CA: 110-134.

Reichl, P., and Hammer, F. (2004), Hot Discussion or Frosty Dialogue? Towards a Temperature Metric for Conversational Interactivity, *International Conference Speech and Language Processing* 1: 317-320.

Resnick, P. (2001), Beyond Bowling Together; SocioTechnical Capital, *in* John M. Carroll (eds.), *Human-Computer Interaction in the New Millennium,* Addison-Wesley, ACM Press, NY.

Riekki, J., Isomursu, P., and Isomursu, M. (2004), Evaluating the calmness of ubiquitous applications, *Proceedings of Production focused Software Process Improvement, 5ᵗʰ International Conference, PROFES 2004,* Kansei Science City, Japan.

Ross, T., and Burnett, G. (2001), Evaluating the human-machine interface to vehicle navigation systems as an example of ubiquitous computing, *International Journal of*

Human-Computer Studies 55: 661-674.

Roth, J. (2002), Patterns of Mobile Interaction, *Personal and Ubiquitous Computing* 6: 282-289.

Roussos, G., and Moussouri, T. (2004), Consumer perceptions of privacy, security and trust in ubiquitous commerce, *Pervasive and ubiquitous Computing* 8: 416-429.

Rubin, J. (1994), *Handbook of Usability testing,* John Wiley, NY.

Russell, D. M., Trimble, J., and Wales, R. (2002), Two paths from the same place: Task driven and human-centered evolution of a group information surface, *Make IT Easy Conference,* San Jose, CA, USA.

Ryu, H., Hong, G. Y., and James, H. (2006), Quality assessment technique for ubiquitous software and middleware, *Res. Lett. Inf. Math. Sci. (Research Letters Information Mathematics Science)* 9: 13-87.

SAIT (2005), *Future life scenarios in ubiquitous service paradigm,* Samsung Advanced Institute of Technology, Internal annual report.

Sako, M., McKenna, C., Molloy, E., and Ventresca, M. (2006), Grand Challenges in Services, *Proceedings of the GCS (Grand Challenges in Services) workshop*, University of Oxford.

Schmidt, A. (2002), *Ubiquitous Computing – Computing in Context,* Ph.D. Dissertation, Lancaster University, UK.

Schmidt, A. (2003-a), Context – Enabling New Ways in Human Computer Interaction, *Workshop on Context-Aware Systems,* Dutch.

Schmidt, A. (2003-b), Interacting with the Ubiquitous Computing, *Proceeding of Mobile HCI 2003,* Italy.

Schneiderman, B. (1998), *Designing the User Interface,* Addison Wesley Inc., California.

Scholtz, J. (2001), Evaluation methods for ubiquitous computing, *UbiComp01 Workshop.*

Scholtz, J. (2003), Application Domains: Government Roles in Human-Computer Interaction, *in* Julie A. Jacko and Andrew Sears (eds.), *The Human-Computer Interaction Handbook,* Lawrence Erlbaum Associates, NJ.

Scholtz, J. (2006), Metrics for Evaluating Human Information Interaction Systems, *Interacting With Computers* 18: 507-527.

Scholtz, J., and Consolvo, S. (2004), Toward a framework for evaluating ubiquitous computing applications, *Pervasive Computing* 3(2): 82-89.

Scholtz, J., Tabassi, E., Consolvo, S., and Schilit, B. (2002), User centered evaluations for ubiquitous computing systems, Best known methods, *UbiComp02, Workshop 2.*

Sears, A. (2003), Testing and Evaluation, *in* Julie A. Jacko and Andrew Sears (eds.), *The Human-Computer Interaction Handbook,* Lawrence Erlbaum Associates, NJ.

Seffah, A., Donyaee, M., Kline, R. B., and Padda, H. K. (2006), Usability measurement and metrics: A consolidated model, *Software Quality Journal* 14: 159-178.

Shackel, B. (1991), Usability - Context, Framework, Definition, Design and Evaluation, *in* B. Shackel and S. Richardson (eds.), *Human Factors for Informatics Usability,* Cambridge University Press.

Shrestha, S., and Kazama, F. (2007), Assessment of surface water quality using multivariate statistical techniques: A case study of the Fuji river basin, Japan, *Environmental Modeling and Software* 22: 464-475.

Siewiorek, D. P. (2002), New frontiers of Application Design, *Communication of the ACM (CACM)* 45: 79-82.

Skiba, B., Johnson, M., and Dillon, M. (2000), *Moving in Mobile Media Mode,* http://www.entsoftware.com.

Smailagic, A., Siewiorek, D. P., Anhalt, J., and Gemperle, F. (2001), Towards context aware computing experiences and lessons, *IEEE Journal on Intelligent Systems* 16.

Snowden, D. J., and Kurtz, C. (2002), Patterns of meaning: Next generation decision support, *IBM Cynefin Center for Organizational Complexity.*

Stanford, V. (2002), Using pervasive computing to deliver elder care, *IEEE Pervasive Computing* 1(1): 10-13.

Steitz, N. A., Tandler, P., Muller-Tomfelde, C., and Konomi, S. (2001), Roomware: Toward the Next Generation of Human-Computer Interaction Based on an Integrated Design of Real and Virtual Worlds, *in* John M. Carroll (eds.), *Human-Computer Interaction in the New Millennium,* Addison-Wesley, ACM Press, NY.

Stephanidis, C., and Savidis, A. (2003), Unified User Interface Development, *in* Julie A. Jacko and Andrew Sears (eds.), *The Human-Computer Interaction Handbook,* Lawrence Erlbaum Associates, NJ.

Svanaes, D. (2000), *Understanding Interactivity; Steps to a Phenomenology of Human-Computer Interaction,* Norwegian University of Science and Technology (NTNU),

Norway.

Sweeney, M., Maguire, M., and Shackel, B. (1993), Evaluating user-computer interaction: a framework, *International Journal of Man-Machine Studies* 38: 689-711.

Takemoto, M., Sunage, H., Tanaka, K., Matsumura, H., and Shinohara, E. (2002), The Ubiquitous Service-Oriented Network (USON) An approach for a ubiquitous world based on P2P technology, *In proceedings 2nd International Conference on Peer-to-Peer Computing.*

Tanaka, Y., Tarumi, T., and Huh, M. H. (1994), Research and Applications of Quantification Methods in East Asian Countries, *in* E. Diday et al. (eds.), *New Approaches in Classification and Data Analysis,* Springer-Verlag, Berlin.

Teas, K. R. (1994), Expectations as a Comparison Standard in Measuring Service Quality: An Assessment of a Reassessment, *Journal of Marketing* 58(1): 132-139.

Teenhaus, M., and Forrest, W. Y. (1985), An analysis and synthesis of multiple correspondence, optimal scaling, dual scaling, homogeneity analysis, and other methods for quantifying categorical multivariate data, *Psychometrika* 50: 429-447.

Thatcher, A. (2006), Information-seeking behaviors and cognitive search strategies in different search tasks on the WWW, *International Journal of Industrial Ergonomics* 36: 1055-1068.

Theodorou, Y., Drossos, C., and Alevizos, P. (2007), Correspondence analysis with fuzzy data: The fuzzy eigenvalue problem, *Fuzzy Sets and Systems* 158: 704-721.

Torres, A., and Velden, M. (2007), Perceptual mapping of multiple variable batteries by plotting supplementary variables in correspondence analysis of rating data, *Food Quality and Preference* 18: 121-129.

Toshio, K. (2005), *u-Japan: From e-Readiness to u-Readiness,* APEC Digital Opportunity Center (ADOC) 2005 week, Session IV: e-Readiness.

Tracy, R. (2001), Evaluating the human-machine interface to vehicle navigation systems as an example of ubiquitous computing, *International Journal of Human-Computer Studies* 55: 661-674.

UbiComp01 (2001), *Evaluation methodologies for ubiquitous computing,* Workshop on Evaluation Methodologies for Ubiquitous Computing.

UbiComp02 (2002), *User-Centered Evaluation of Ubiquitous Computing Application,* Workshop on User-Centered Evaluation of Ubiquitous Computing Application.

Vergo, J., Noronha, S., Kramer, J., Lechner, J., and Cofino, T. (2003), Application Domains: e-Commerce Interface Design, *in* Julie A. Jacko and Andrew Sears (eds.), *The Human-Computer Interaction Handbook,* Lawrence Erlbaum Associates, NJ.

Vredenburg, K. (2002), *User Engineering: an overview,* IBM Technical reports.

Wang, Z., and Garlan, D. (2000), *Task-Driven Computing, AURA Project report (CMU-CS-00-154),* School of Computer Science, Carnegie Mellon University, PA, USA.

Want, R., Borriello, G., Pering, T., and Farkas, K. (2002), Disappearing Hardware, *IEEE Pervasive computing* Jan.-Mar.: 36-47.

Watson, R. T., Pitt, L. F., and Kavan, C. B. (1998), Measuring Information Systems Service Quality: Lessons from Two Longitudinal Case Studies, *MIS Quarterly* 22(1): 61-79.

Westwater, M. G., and Johnson, G. I. (1995), Comparing heuristic, user-centered and checklist-based evaluation approaches, *in* Robertson, S. A. (eds.), *Contemporary Ergonomics,* Taylor & Francis, London.

Williams, J. R. (2004), *Developing Performance Support for Computer Systems: a Strategy for Maximizing Usability and Learnability,* CRC Press.

Won, W. H., and Lee, J. H. (2007), Interactivity and Interaction: Proposing a New Measurement of Online Advertising Effectiveness, *Korean Association for Advertising and Public Relations* 9(1): 223-249.

Wu, G. (1999), Perceived Interactivity and Attitude toward Websites, *Annual Conference of the American Academy of Advertising in Albuquerque,* New Mexico.

Wu, M. L., and Wang, Y. S. (2007), Using chemometrics to evaluate anthropogenic effects in Daya Bay, China, *Estuarine, Coastal and Shelf Science* 72: 732-742.

Yadav, M. S., and Varadarajan, R. (2005), Interactivity in the Electronic Marketplace: An Exposition of the Concept and Implications for Research, *Journal of the Academy of Marketing Science* 33: 585-603.

Yamazaki, K. (2004), Research Directions for Ubiquitous Services, *In Proceedings of international Symposium on Applications and the Internet (SAINT).*

Yeo, C. K., Lee, B. S., and Er, M. H. (2004), A survey of application level multicast techniques, *Computer Communications* 27: 1547-1568.

Zack, M. H. (1993), Interactivity and Communication mode choice in ongoing management groups, *Information Systems Research* 4(3): 207-239.

Zucker, A., McGhee, R., Hall, C., Hersh, L., Nielsen, N., and Penuel, B. (2006), Exemplary Technology-Supported Schooling Case Studies: Evaluating the impact of ubiquitous computing in K-12 schools, *SRI International Project,* NSF (National Science Foundation).

Part V: Appendix

[Appendix A] Example: Index/factor for interactivity

A.1 Interactivity dimension (Muirhead, 2001)

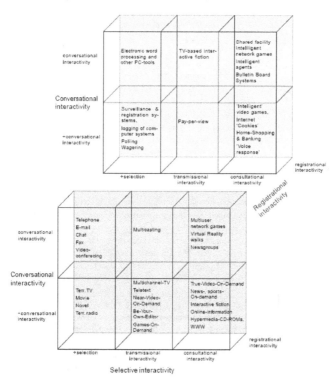

A.2 Level of interactivity (Rafaeli, 1998)

1. Object Interactivity	This refers to an application in which objects such as buttons, people, and things are activated by using a mouse or other pointing device. When a user clicks on the object, there will be some form of audio-visual response. This seems to be the most pervasive, common type of interactivity that we encounter on the internet.
2. Linear Interactivity	Refers to applications in which the user is able to move forward or backwards through a pre-determined linear sequence. This is often termed electronic page turning. This type of interaction does not provide for response-specific feedback to learner actions. In fact, this class of interactivity lends itself to Manovich's criticism where the user has to accept someone else's mental associations in experiencing the content of the sequence.
3. Support Interactivity	An essential component of any software application is the ability to receive performance support. It could range from a small help or FAQs section to a complex tutorial system.
4. Update Interactivity	One of the more powerful classes of interactivity as it relates to initiating dialogue between the learner and the computer-generated content. Here, the application generates a problem (from a database) to which the learner must respond. The analysis of the response results in a computer-generated update or feedback. Update interactivity can range from a simple question and answer format to complex conditional responses. We also tend to find this on the internet on websites where there are games to play or mysteries to solve, i.e. if, user does this, then do this, else do that. However, more often than note, this type of interactivity is more commonly found on educational multimedia applications designed for courses, companies, etc. for their employees to train or their students to learn.
5. Construct Interactivity	The construct class of interactivity is an extension of update interactivity. It requires the creation of an instructional environment in which the learner is required to manipulate component objects to achieve specific goals. Unless the construction is completed in the correct sequence, the task cannot be completed.
6. Reflective Interactivity	It records each response entered by the users of the application and allows them to compare their response to that of other users as well as recognized experts. In this way, learners can reflect on their own response and make their own judgment as to its accuracy or correctness.
7. Simulation Interactivity	It extends the role of the learner to that of controller or operator, where individual selections determine the training sequence. The simulation and construct interactivity levels are closely linked and may require the learner to complete a specific sequence of tasks before a suitable update can be generated. For example, the simulation may be controlled and the learner only progresses after making a correct choice.
8. Hyperlinked Interactivity	The learner has access to a wealth of information and may travel at will through that knowledge base. To me, this seems like interactivity on its

185

	most basic level. You are interacting with the environment, true, but only on the most elemental level.
9. Non-immersive Contextual Interactivity	This concept combines and extends the various interactive levels into a complete virtual training environment. Rather than taking a passive role in which they work through a series of content-oriented sequences, they are transported into a new world which models their existing work environment and the tasks they undertake reflect those of the work experience. For example, one could probably take a virtual trip on an 18th century warship and interact with the crew as they encounter them.
10. Immersive Virtual Interactivity	Often perceived as the 'ultimate' in interaction. It provides an interactive environment in which the learner is projected into a complete computer-generated world which responds to individual movement and actions.

A.3 Mobile interactivity (Lee, 2003)

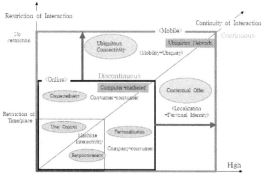

[Appendix B] Example: Index/factor for ubiquitous service evaluation

B.1 UbiComp workshop on evaluation method (2001; 2002)

Index	Definition	Metrics	Challenge for evaluation
Universality	For who and applicable domain	· Personal info · Training	· New class of users: non desktop · New uses cases: workload, metrics, stress points aren't identified, no reference points
Utility	Benefit to users metrics	· Inferencing	· Situated interaction: physical interactions · Problem: what data do we need to capture, how can that data be captured, evaluation technologies for system in use, multimodal I/O
Usability	Effort/Utility unit	· Configuration · Predictability · Distraction · Mixed initiative · Cost of reversing a decision	· Task appropriate interactions · How do we capture user intent?, finer grain attention analysis
Ubiquity	Points of delivery in physical world (where) and when	· Graceful degradation · Trust	· Ubiquitous · Larger set of degraded operating modes

B.2 Ryu et al. (2006)

Objects	Component	Sub-component	Evaluation questions
User	Activities	Predictability (Feed-forward)	· Can users predict or understand what is required as input data and what is provided as output by the ubiquitous systems?
		Accountability	· Can users understand how the current states of the system were provided as output by the ubiquitous systems?
		Simplicity	· How long does the user take to use activities correctly?
	Evaluation	Reversibility	· Can user easily correct errors on tasks?
		Acknowledgement	· Can user easily understand message from the ubiquitous systems? · Is the information useful and relevant to the users?

I/O Artifacts	Reception	Quality of reception	· How often does the user succeed to exchange data between target and other component?
			· Are differences between the actual and reasonable expected results acceptable?
		Mobility	· Is the device easily mobile?
			· Is the device transparently passed between sink nodes in the system?
	Integration	Ubiquitous connectivity and integrity	· Are the physical artifacts seamlessly connected?
			· How wide range does the ubiquitous computing system take coverage?
	Expression	Transparency	· Does the output artifact add minimal cognitive load?
		Unobtrusiveness	· How much attention does the user have to pay in order to command their activities?
		Awareness support	· Does user ever fail to watch when encountering important message?
Services	Functionality	Compliance	· How compliant is the functionality of the product to applicable regulations, standards and conventions?
		Suitability	· How adequate are the evaluated functions?
		Accuracy	· Are the differences between the actual and reasonably expected results acceptable?
	Service quality	Efficiency	· What is the time taken to complete a task?
		Reliability	· How to measure system reliability?
	Contextuali-zation	Location-awareness	· How accurate can the ubiquitous computing system sense the user location?
		Environment-awareness	· Is the system capable of providing environment-aware, such as location-aware and orientation-aware sensor data?
	Security and privacy	Privacy	· How complete is the audit concerning the user access to the system and data?
Systems software	Configuration	Scalability	· Does the ubiquitous computing system support the ability to add new hardware, software or users?
		Security	· Does the system software logically separate user requests?
	Coordination	Resource coordination and optimization	· How well does the systems software control resource sharing on the local hardware?
		Mobility	· Is the resource monitoring aspect of the systems software sophisticated enough to judge whether a program or code would be more efficient if located elsewhere?

B.3 Scholtz and Consolvo (2004)

UEA	Metric	Conceptual measures
Attention	Focus	· Number of times a user needs to change focus due to technology · Number of different displays or actions a user needs to reference to accomplish an interaction or to check on the progress of an interaction · Number of events not noticed by a user in an acceptable time · Workload imposed on the user attributable to focus
Adoption	Rate	· New users and/or unit of time · Adoption rationale · Technology usage statistics
	Value	· Change(s) in productivity · Perceived cost and benefit · Continuity for user · Amount of customer sacrifice
	Availability	· Number of actual users from each target user group · Technology supply source · Categories of users in post-deployment
Trust	Privacy	· Amount of information user has to divulge to obtain value from application · Availability of explanations to user about use of recorded data
	Awareness	· Ease of coordination with others in multi-user application · Number of collisions with activities of others
Conceptual Models	Predictability of application behavior	· Degree of match between user's model and actual behavior of the application
	Awareness of application capability(ies)	· Degree of match between user's model and actual functionality of the application
	Vocabulary-awareness	· Degree of match between user's model and the syntax of multimodal interactions
Interaction	Effectiveness	· Percentage of task completion
	Efficiency	· Time to complete a task
	User Satisfaction	· User rating of performing the task
	Distraction	· Time taken from the primary task · Degradation of performance in primary task · Level of user frustration
	Interaction transparency	· Effectiveness comparisons on different sets of input or output devices
	Collaborative interaction	· Number of conflicts · Percentage of conflicts resolved by the application · User feelings about conflicts and how they are resolved · User ability to recover from conflicts

Invisibility	Intelligibility	· User understands of the system explanation
	Control	· Effectiveness of interactions provided for user control of system initiative
	Accuracy	· Match between the system's contextual model and the actual situation
	Appropriateness of action	· Match between the system action and the action the user would have requested
	Customization	· Time to explicitly enter personalization information or time for the system to learn and adapt to the user's preferences
Impact	Behavior changes	· Type, frequency and duration · Match between user's current job description and application role
	Social acceptance	· Requirements placed on user outside of social norms
	Environment change	· Type, frequency and duration

B.4 Lewis (2002)

Overall	Overall I am satisfied with how easy it is to use this system
System usefulness	· It was simple to use this system · I could effectively complete the tasks and scenarios using this system · I was able to complete the tasks and scenarios quickly using this system · I was able to efficiently complete the tasks and scenarios using this system · I felt comfortable using this system · It was easy to learn to use this system · I believe I could become productive quickly using this system
Information quality	· The system gave error message that clearly told me how to fix problems · Whenever I made a mistake using the system, I could recover easily and quickly · The information (such as on-line help, on-screen message and other documentation) provided with this system was clear · It was easy to find the information I needed · The information provided for the system was easy to understand · The information was effective in helping me complete the tasks and scenarios · The organization of information on the system screens was clear
Interface quality	· The interface of this system was pleasant · I liked using the interface of this system · This system has all the functions and capabilities I expect it to have
Overall	· Overall I am satisfied with this system

B.5 Ubiquitous service usability factor (Kim, 2006)

Factor	Questionnaire examples
Accountability	· The exterior of this service (system) will seem neat and clean
Ability	· This service (system) will perform the wanted service well at once
Sustainability	· This service (system) will always help me to the utmost
Trust	· This service (system) will not drive me into a corner
Efficiency	· This service (system) will be supplied promptly
Learnability	· The manual of this service (system) will be easy to learn
Memorability	· The manual of this service (system) will be easy to memorize
Error prevention	· This service (system) will hardly make errors
Communication	· This service (system) will recognize my order or command well
Context awareness	· It will be good if this system fathoms my mind and makes the service that I did not ordered
Mobility	· It will be convenient that the kinds of service are confined to those suitable to the place
Scalability	· The service contents will be automatically adjusted according to my habit and taste
Customization	· This service will recognize me (owner) and put my desire at the top priority
Authorization	· This service (system) will be able to be stopped or changed by me at any time
Feedback	· If the kind of service and its process status are informed continuously, it will be annoying
Predictability	· The service must be served so naturally that the service cannot be felt
Utility	· The serving way of service will be kind and comfortable
Fun	· This service (system) will make my space of life more pleasant
Safety	· This service (system) will make me uneasy because it seems to know my private life
Accessibility	· If I know how this service is supplied, I will use the service more comfortably
Overall satisfaction	· This service will be helpful in leading the satisfactory life

B.6 Usability checklist (ISO 9241-9/11, 1998; ISO 9126-1~4, 2001)

ISO 9126-1	Quality in use	· The capability of the software product to enable specified users to achieve specified goals with effectiveness, productivity, safety and satisfaction in specified contexts of use
	Functionality	· The capability of the software product to provide functions which meet stated and implied needs when the software is used under specified conditions · Accuracy, Suitability, Interoperability, Security
	Reliability	· The capability of the software product to maintain a specified level of performance when used under specified conditions · Maturity, Fault tolerance, Recoverability, Availability

	Usability	· The capability of the software product to be understood, learned, used and attractive to the user, when used under specified conditions · Understandability, Learnability, Operability
	Efficiency	· The capability of the software product to provide appropriate performance, relative to the amount of resources used, under stated conditions · Time behavior, Resource, Utilization
	Maintainability	· The capability of the software product to be modified · Analyzability, Chageability, Stability, Testability
	Protability	· The capability of the software product to be transferred from one environment to another · Adaptability, Installabillity, Co-existence, Replaceability
ISO 9241-11	Guideline on usability	
	Usability	· The extent to which a product can be used by specified users to achieve specified goals with effectiveness, efficiency and satisfaction in a specified context o use
	Effectiveness	· The accuracy and completeness with which users achieve specified goals
	Efficiency	· The resources expended in relation to the accuracy and completeness with which users achieve goals, mean transaction times
	Satisfaction	· The comfort and acceptability of use, SUMI questionnaire

[Appendix C] Basic statistics analysis

The following results illustrated the data reduction technique in 3.3 sections.

C.1 Principal Component Analysis (PCA)

For Principal Component Analysis (PCA), SAS 6.0 was used. Through the rotation method of Varimax with Kaiser Normalization, it was repeated sixteen times. As PCA is a method to set the indicator by catching the expositive degree of variables with the eigenvalue lager than 1, we defined the variables with the expositive capacity of 80% among the values with eigenvalue of more than 1 on the basis of results. Figure C-1 shows the PCA results. The figure on the left shows the Scree plot, where the variables with eigenvalue larger than 1 are five. However, as the increase of main component number and the expositive capacity are proportional, only the main components with the expositive capacity of 80% or more are selected for the proper trade-off (four components; cumulative expositive capacity: 79.3%). Hence, the fifth main component was excluded, even though its eigenvalue was larger than 1.

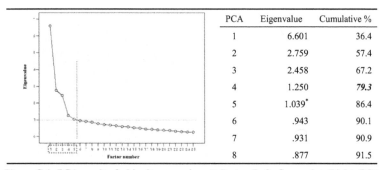

PCA	Eigenvalue	Cumulative %
1	6.601	36.4
2	2.759	57.4
3	2.458	67.2
4	1.250	*79.3*
5	1.039*	86.4
6	.943	90.1
7	.931	90.9
8	.877	91.5

Figure C-1. PCA result of ubiquitous service attributes (Left: Scree plot, Right: PCA results) (*: Though the eigenvalue is more than 1, only 4 main components are selected on the basis of 80% expositive capacity)

Table C-1. PCA result related to ubiquitous service attributes (verimax rotation)

	Factors	PCA 1	PCA 2	PCA 3	PCA 4	PCA 5
Contextualization support	Real time connectivity	*.810*	.051	.081	.162	.097
	Ubiquitous connectivity	*.780*	.145	.007	.088	.032
	Portability	*.753*	.110	-.060	.044	.163
	Ubiquity	*.715*	.153	.125	.057	-.056
	Mobility	*.672*	-.034	.306	.124	-.066
	Accessibility	*.599*	-.086	.000	.165	.379
	Context-awareness	*.554*	.152	.270	-.006	.310
	Location-awareness	*.523*	.144	.401	-.063	-.147
	Universality	*.491*	-.305	.277	.134	.267
Service capability support	Application robustness	.072	*.744*	.080	.024	.029
	Compliance	.039	*.738*	.245	.083	-.011
	System capability	.160	*.706*	-.036	-.049	.232
	Linking to other systems	.053	*.674*	.123	.027	.314
	Service assurance	.159	*.352*	.077	.016	.600
	Functionality	.100	*.480*	.092	.095	.599
Ubiquity support	Suitability	.226	.169	*.650*	.181	.074
	Predictability	-.068	.212	*.645*	.312	.040
	Safety	.292	.082	*.642*	-.111	.157
	Personalization	.100	-.090	*.565*	.473	.165
	Feedback/feed-forward	.130	.097	*.531*	.400	.243
	Security	.019	.142	*.415*	.220	.604
User experience support	Learnability	.083	.018	.154	*.813*	.011
	Understandability	-.067	.104	.276	*.721*	.010
	Distraction	.311	-.028	-.121	*.659*	.051
	Usability	.195	.001	.232	*.424*	.242

Each factor was adjusted to contain only the indicators of which the factor loading was larger than .5 (Shrestha and Kazama, 2007). From the result of analysis of main components (table C-1), we classified the ubiquitous service attributes into four groups and defined their characteristics as follows:

- Contextualization support: related to the ubiquitous service environment
- Service Capability support: related to the supplying capacity of ubiquitous service
- Ubiquity support: related to the ubiquity of ubiquitous service
- User experience support: related to the user's experience of the supplied u-Service

C.2 Correspondence Analysis (CA)

For the structuring of the evaluation indicators, we made the Correspondence Analysis (CA) to analyze the relation among the derived main indicators of attributes. To maintain the consistency of indicator derivation, we made the second examination the ten participants of factor analysis and main component analysis (ordered of the ubiquitous service, policy planner, designer, developer, related standard researcher, etc.).

The correspondence analysis used to analyze the relation among the finally selected indicators was developed and used in diverse names. It is called the optimal scaling in America, the dual scaling in Canada, the homogeneity analysis in Holland, and the quantification III-type analysis method in Japan. Among the statisticians and psycho-statisticians, it has been introduced in different names such as reciprocal averaging, canonical correlation analysis of contingency table, and categorical discriminant analysis (Greenancre, 1984; Teenhaus and Forrest, 1985). In this study, we made the correspondence analysis through the quantification III-type analysis method, which was verified in the field of affective engineering, human factors (ergonomics), HCI department. Thus, the I/O responses which the response pattern of the evaluators showed against the p stimuli were used as the basic data for the analysis (Johnson and Wichern, 1988; Theodorou et al., 2007).

The correspondence analysis is a kind of Multi-Dimensional Scaling (MDS) that has the purpose of giving the proper quantified values to the row range and the line range, expressing the two variable sets on one perception map.

Table C-2. Details of correspondence analysis (Degree of freedom = 42)

Dimension	Eigenvalue	Chi-square	Percentages	Cumulative percentages
1	.14384	1.79126	77.30	77.30
2	.06037	.31548	13.61	*90.92*
3	.04931	.21048	9.08	100.00

As it expresses the information of a different set of variables on a two- or three-dimensional coordinates, the information of corresponding variables are closely shown in a group type. Thus, it expresses the dependent variables and subjects which are to be observed on the one perception map as the MDS. This method had been used in geometrically interpreting the data in multidimensional spaces, and more recently it is widely used in the marketing areas to analyze the attributes of diverse product sets, as well as in the recognition science, psychology, industrial engineering, and human factors (ergonomics) etc. (Hoffman and George, 1986; Riekki et al., 2004; Yeo et al., 2004; Mankoff and Carter, 2005).

The data form used in this study was the rectangular data matrix, and the contents on the attributes were analyzed through the PCA results. All the persons who had participated in the first research participated in the second one, as well. The related item was indicated as '1' and the unrelated was as '0', in a completed a relation matrix. This matrix was used as the input data for the multi-response analysis. SAS 6.0 was used for it, and the data from ten participants were mobilized. The result of the response analysis is shown in table C-2.

In table, the expositive capacity of first dimension is about 77%, and the expositive capacity of second dimension is about 13%. As a result, the total expositive capacity of two dimensions is as high as 90.92%. The values of variables in each dimension are shown in table C-3.

Table C-3 shows the values of the first and second dimension axes for the interactivity attributes in the ubiquitous service environment. The 'quality' shows how far the variables can be explained with the current two axes. With these two axes, the contextualization support can be explained by 99% and the capability support by 93%. But the attributes of fun and reliability showed a low expositive capacity of less than 10%. The 'mass' means the ratio of each row to the total sum. Both of the attributes showed the even ratios. The 'inertia' means the importance of each row, and shows the result similar to the analysis result of PCA (Hair et al., 1998).

Table C-3. Variables coordinates and statistics for the points

	Variables	Statistics for the points			Partial contributions to inertia for the points	
		Quality	Mass	Inertia	Dim. 1	Dim. 2
Row coordinates	Contextualization support	.9914	.2371	.4850	.6017	.1153
	Service capability support	.9349	.2541	.1064	.0131	.6565
	Ubiquity support	.7835	.2563	.1636	.1256	.2282
	User experience support	.8191	.2525	.2450	.2596	.0000
Column coordinates	Efficiency	.9378	.0693	.0820	.0876	.0675
	Effectiveness	.9999	.0660	.0533	.0230	.2604
	Satisfaction	.9990	.0594	.0353	.0006	.2556
	Responsiveness	.8601	.0743	.0566	.0595	.0192
	Help or Wizard	.6372	.0660	.0627	.0476	.0230
	Connectivity	.9121	.0660	.0636	.0749	.0004
	Unobtrusiveness	.9949	.0677	.0772	.0993	.0004
	Leanability	.9885	.0594	.0885	.1116	.0084
	Level of effort	.9885	.0677	.1984	.2530	.0041
	User controllability	.9990	.0001	.1165	.1506	.0001
	User involvement	.9598	.0726	.0643	.0739	.0337
	Reality	.7250	.0627	.0504	.0048	.2410
	Fun	.0921	.0693	.0173	.0018	.0017
	Experienceability	.8572	.0660	.0236	.0118	.0820
	Reliability	.0327	.0660	.0104	.0000	.0025

The partial contribution is the concept similar to the factor loadage of factor analysis, and shows the relational degree of each dimension and level. Here, the attributes close to the dimension 1 were the service capability support and the utility support. The reliability and the fun turned out to be low-related to the present dimension (Torres and Velden, 2007).

Moreover, we made the correspondence analysis to structurize the response of participants on the perception map. When results of the correspondence analysis were expressed on the perception map, we obtained figure C-2. As shown in the figure, the ubiquitous service attributes were clearly distinguished in four different fields. And the main component and related correspondent attribute were shown as follows.

197

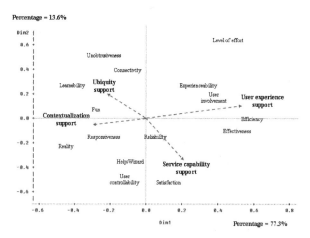

Figure C-2. Correspondence analysis: Conceptual map of the attributes

By integrating the results of main component analysis and correspondence analysis, we got the result of association analysis as shown in the figure. Based on the result, we proceeded the structuring of indicators. The peculiar point in the result is that the ubiquitous service attributes and the interactivity attributes in the ubiquitous environment are overlapped in many parts. Especially, the 'contextualization support' in the ubiquitous service attributes and the 'ubiquity support' in the interactivity attributes is very similar to each other. This point should be considered when the indicators of questionnaire are composed. The significance of each factor can be calculated through the inertia, but the inertia in the correspondence analysis is just a result of correlation between the corresponding components. Hence, in this study, we estimated the importance of each factor through the experimental analysis for more accurate calculation.

[Appendix D] Example: Performance measurement indicator

D.1 Ryu et al. (2006)

Attribute	Metric
Predictability	· A/B · A: Number of input and output items which user successfully understands and predicts · B: Number of input and output items available from the ubiquitous interface · 1-(A/B) · A: Number of message or functions which user found unacceptably inconsistent with user's expectation · B: Number of messages or functions · N/UOT · N: Number of operations which user found unacceptably inconsistent with the user's expectation · UOT: User Operating Time (during observation period)
Accountability	· A/B · A: Number of approval event · B: Number of autonomous situation where there are competing context · A/B · A: Number of trials which user successfully found system help/support · B: Number of trials to access to system help or support
Simplicity	· Mean number of steps to activities
Reversibility	· A/UOT · A: Number of times that the user succeeds to cancel their error operation · UOT: User Operating Time (during observation period)
Acknowledgement	· A/UOT · A: Number of times that the user pauses for a long period or successively and repeatedly fails at the same operation, because of the lack of message comprehension · UOT: User Operating Time (during observation period)
Quality of reception	· A/B · A: Number of cases in which user succeeded to exchange data with other systems · B: Number of cases in which user attempted to exchange data
Mobility	· A/B · A: Number of successful device handovers · B: Number of attempts to handover
Ubiquitous connectivity and integrity	· Count the number of events where the physical artifacts did not receive the data from the system, considering the system specification on communication coverage

Transparency	· Effectiveness comparisons on different sets of I/O devices
Unobtrusiveness	· A/UOT
	· A: Number of times that the user starting at the input or output artifacts to trigger their next activities
	· UOT: User Operating Time (during observation period)
Awareness support	· Number of collisions with activities of others
Controllability	· T/N
	· T: Operation time period during observation
	· N: Number of occurrence of user's human error operation
Compliance	· Success rate: the percentage of test cases that passed at the last execution = number of failed test cases/total number of test cases
Suitability	· Function adequacy X=A/B
	· A: Number of functions in which problems are detected
	· B: Total number of functions
Accuracy	· A/T
	· A: Number of cases encountered by the users with a difference against the reasonably expected results beyond allowable
	· T: Operation time
Efficiency	· Response time T = (time of gaining the result) − (time of command entry finished)
Fault recovery	· A/B
	· A: Number of implemented recovery requirements confirmed
	· B: Number of recovery requirements in the specification

D.2 Constantine and Lockwood (1999)

Essential metric index	Metric
Essential efficiency	· EE=$100 \times$ (Essential/Enacted)
Task concordance	· TC=$100 \times$(D/P)
	· D: Discordance score = number of pairs of tasks ranked in correct order by enacted length less number of pairs out of order
	· P: Number of possible task pairs
Task visibility	· TV=$100 \times (1/\text{Total}) \times \sum V_i$
	· Total: Total number of enacted steps to complete use cases
	· V: Feature visibility (0 to 1) of enacted step i
Layout uniformity	· LU=$100 \times$(1-(heights, widths, top-edge alignments, left-edge alignments, bottom-edge alignments, right-edge alignments)-M)/($6 \times$N-M)
	· N: Total number of visual components on screen
	· M: Adjustment for the minimum number of possible alignments and sizes need to make the value of LU range from 0 to 100

D.3 Bertoa et al. (2006)

Attribute	Indicator	Derived measure
Contents of manuals	· Manuals coverage	· % of Functional Elements (FE) described in manuals
		· % of interfaces described in manuals
		· % of methods described in manuals
		· % of configurable parameters described in manuals
	· Manuals consistency	· % of FE incorrectly described in manuals
		· Component version difference
	· Manuals legibility	· Ratio of HTML files of manuals per FE
		· Ratio of figures per kilo-word
Size of manuals	· Manuals suitability	· Ratio of words per FE
		· Ratio of words per interface
		· Ratio of words per method
		· Ratio of words per configurable parameter
Effectiveness of manuals	· Effectiveness ratio	· % of FE correctly used after reading the manuals
Contents of demos	· Demos coverage	· Percentage of FE included in demos
	· Demos consistency	· Demo version difference
Contents of marketing information	· Information coverage	· Number of FE in marketing information
	· Information consistency	· Marketing information version difference

D.4 Scholtz (2006)

Factor	Metric
Analyst time	· # queries system augments appropriately
	· # of misspellings, alternative spellings, ambiguities system handles
	· Match of automatic decomposition of problem with human decomposition
	· # tasks system anticipates
	· % system recommendations accepted by analyst
	· Reading time to understand set of documents
	· Time to recover from interruptions
Data coverage	· % knowledge gaps closed by system
	· % relevant documents returned
	· Time to recognize gaps in knowledge
	· Ease of recognizing gaps
Analysis process	· Redirection of automated resources
	· Interoperability of tools
	· Parallel efforts managed
	· # subtasks reduced
	· # additional tasks created by the software
Analysis facilitation	· Software usage

	· User satisfaction
	· Insights gained
	· Perceived effort
Product quality	· Expert judgment of coverage
	· Customer satisfaction with product

D.5 ISO 9241-11 (1998)

Component	Relevant data
Users characteristics	· Psychological attributes including cognitive style
Task characteristics	· Frequency, duration and importance, task flexibility or pacing, physical and mental demands
Technical environment characteristic	· Hardware capabilities and constraints · Network connection, operating system, supporting software
Physical environment	· Noise level, privacy, ambient qualities, potential health hazards, safety issues
Organizational environment	· Structure of the operational teams and the individual staff members' level of autonomy · Work and safety policies, organizational culture, feedback to employees on job quality
Social environment	· Multi-or single-user environment, degree of assistance available

D.6 Basu et al. (2001)

No	Metric
1	Number of devices in the network-this relates to area density, richness of network connectivity.
2	Number of devices that need to participate in a particular application (number of).
3	Complexity of relationships between nodes of the resource graph of an application (number of edges in the resource graph, structure of the resource graph-whether it is a tree or not).
4	Number of instances of resources in the UbiComp network with similar capabilities or attributes.
5	Number of different task instances (of same or different tasks) running simultaneously on the UbiComp network.
6	Fraction of the devices in the network that rely on a wireless access point for routing (rest use ad hoc routing).
7	Average data rate required by the distributed application.
8	Background traffic patterns ranging from low load to heavy load.
9	Mobility patterns of users and other service providing devices ranging from random to highly predictable. Particular parameters in this context are: speed of motion, frequency and duration of pauses in mobility.

www.ingramcontent.com/pod-product-compliance
Lightning Source LLC
LaVergne TN
LVHW022310060326
832902LV00020B/3377